Shatter the System

Shatter the System

Equity Leadership and Social Justice Advocacy in Education

Candice Dowd Maxwell

ROWMAN & LITTLEFIELD
Lanham • Boulder • New York • London

Published by Rowman & Littlefield
An imprint of The Rowman & Littlefield Publishing Group, Inc.
4501 Forbes Boulevard, Suite 200, Lanham, Maryland 20706
www.rowman.com

86-90 Paul Street, London EC2A 4NE

Copyright © 2022 by Candice Dowd Maxwell

All rights reserved. No part of this book may be reproduced in any form or by any electronic or mechanical means, including information storage and retrieval systems, without written permission from the publisher, except by a reviewer who may quote passages in a review.

British Library Cataloguing in Publication Information Available

Library of Congress Cataloging-in-Publication Data Available

ISBN: 978-1-4758-6449-6 (cloth)
ISBN: 978-1-4758-6450-2 (paper)
ISBN: 978-1-4758-6451-9 (electronic)

Contents

Preface	vii
Acknowledgments	xi
Introduction	1
PART I: WHY THIS BOOK, AND WHY NOW?	3
Chapter 1: The Effects of Social Conditioning on Education	7
Chapter 2: Definitions and Terms	21
Chapter 3: Equity Leadership and Social Justice Advocacy	31
Chapter 4: Humility, Diversity, Equity, and Inclusion (HDEI) Framing	45
PART II: EQUITABLE-SOCIAL CHANGE PROCESS MODEL	65
Chapter 5: Awareness and Affirmation	67
Chapter 6: Allyship, Advocacy, Access, and Activism	89
Chapter 7: Accountability and Auditing	97
Chapter 8: Commitment to Practice and Closing	103
About the Author	111

Preface

At some point, we need to find a new historical precipice in American education to climb that capitalizes on the strength of our changing demography. It is quite possible that we have lingered and lamented in the valley far too long, hoping that the mirage of equality would turn into a reality.

Could it be that we have been doing the same thing or refreshing old ideas and giving those ideas new names while continuing to maintain the status quo? Quite possibly, we are attempting, in vain, to signify that we honor diversity without practicing equity and that is a false flag of social change within education that needs to be examined and remedied.

This book is an examination of the challenges we have faced historically in education and how those challenges have persisted into our contemporary existence. However, *Shatter the System* is also written for those who are looking to operationalize equity in their respective spaces and center equity in their lives—to shift their ideologies, implement change, and evaluate the impact of that change. This book is written for those who are ready to have a different conversation that starts with equity first to realize true equality for all.

In this book, I will argue that focusing on equity will allow us to truly experience representation and equality, which are terms commonly used to describe diversity. It will be through those who make a commitment to practice, not simply make a declaration of the issues that will position educators to implement the necessary shifts for social justice advocacy and change. A primary shift during the process of centering and advancing equity is the type of conversations individuals are engaging in that moves from awareness to action, and leverage diversity for inclusion and equity in their respective spaces.

A second shift will promote humility as foundational to ensure students of all backgrounds, family incomes, races, and religions can finally experience access without barriers and obstacles. It is through the activation of humility that authentic stories are elevated and the voice of historically underrepresented individuals and other people from marginalized groups are expressed and not policed. A third shift will focus on the move from advocacy to activism, and the final shift will measure the degree to which the collective work of the allyship is effective, equitable, and transformational.

As you explore this book, race, education, equity, and humility are unapologetically woven throughout each part. While race has always been polarizing and uncomfortable to discuss, the question that we must ask ourselves is why. Why is race such an uncomfortable topic? Why do we continue to have these conversations about race, and what are these conversations doing to effect change? I would offer a few points in response to those questions.

One, perhaps we continue to have the conversation because we have not normalized race talk as a regular part of our lives to acknowledge the complete history of race and institutional racism and oppression in America. Two, perhaps we need to have a different conversation. I would argue that what we have been attempting to do for centuries is work within and navigate systems of inequality in search of equality. There have been many successful and failed attempts to build upon compromised democratic foundations. These attempts have allowed a few people to find success, while others remain at a disadvantage.

Some individuals who might identify with an underrepresented and marginalized group could conceivably have navigated the system better than others could. Still, those individuals faced enormous racialized and unnecessary struggles, challenges, triggers, and traumas that those from the perceived aspirational-dominant culture have not experienced. By aspirational-dominant culture, I am referring to whiteness and a social and cultural construct. This concept will be defined and discussed in later chapters, as it relates to tertiary oppression.

At some point, we have to shift our conversations from navigating systems of inequalities to dismantling those systems and redesigned policies, not just practices, which will expose the inequities and open more doors for more people to have access to resources, information, and opportunities. I am unsure if we have reached that point, but that should remain the overall goal and vision of equity leaders and social justice advocates.

Each one of us is the sinful offspring of legitimized systems of oppression—systems pampered by privilege and power like a manicured mistress. It is time to finally excavate the truth and shatter the system so that moving forward is built on sustainable outcomes of equity and not the status quo that has historically excluded many people in this country from enjoying full access to a wide-open future.

Third, we have only attempted to do something different to remedy the social ills for a short period of time in history. Some of the shifts that are necessary can happen much faster. Some things will take a little more time, and some of what people are experiencing will require a change of heart and ideology, not just a change in policy. A change of heart and ideology is a much more difficult shift. That level of shifting will require individuals to engage in some deep unpacking of biases, discriminatory patterns of beliefs, to develop new habits of thinking and behaving.

Lastly, I would argue that collectively, those who have been fighting for social justice and equity have been working in the background, offline, out of sight and mind for the last few decades. Their tireless efforts have not always penetrated those with the positions and power to make the change real. Therefore, the conversation continues in peril. We can critique the system and make demands for equity. We can hold those in position and power accountable for implementing the change needed, and we can implicate ourselves in doing the work. Most importantly, we must work together and build authentic relationships to honor each other's humanity and dignity. Equity work fails in a silo. We need individuals coming together to make small and big, sweeping, substantive changes.

After reading this book, the hope is that you will:

- consider your position as an equity leader or social justice advocate in your school or organization to influence thoughts, behaviors, and actions;
- discuss the information in this book with other individuals who are interested in leveraging their privilege, position, and power for

historically and traditionally underrepresented and marginalized individuals and groups of people; and
- use the equitable and social change process model (ESCP) to engage in diagnosing issues of equity and redesign systems to eliminate discriminatory practices, programming, ideologies, and policies within education.

Acknowledgments

To those who never allowed me to shrink to fit inside a box that other people may have created for their comfort, thank you! I continue to be encouraged, motivated, and inspired to live a life of divine expectations, even when the earth moves beneath my feet, my steps are uncertain, and the consequences of my decisions are unknown and fragile. With your love and support, I push forward in a continuous effort for self-improvement and social change.

This book is dedicated to every little girl and boy of color who needs an ally—an ally who is committed to equity and will leverage their position, privilege, and power for justice, access, and equity. This is for ancestors who used their voices, gifts, talents, and experiences to challenge systems, to stand in the gap, and continue to insist that we achieve equity.

Shatter the System is a call to action for all of us to implicate ourselves in building a strong and steady bridge across which the next generation of humanity can walk into the promised land of the American Dream, without obstacles and barriers blocking their pathways.

Introduction

HOW THIS BOOK IS ORGANIZED

Shatter the System: Equity Leadership and Social Justice Advocacy in Education is organized into two parts. Part I is composed of the first four chapters of this book. These chapters set the foundation for educational equity in a twenty-first-century system that is primed for social justice, reform, and substantive change. Chapter 1 provides context, while chapter 2 defines terms and movements discussed in later chapters. In chapter 3, the reader will read about the roles, responsibilities, and power of equity leaders, leadership, and social justice advocates to implement change.

Part II of this book, chapters 5 through 8, introduces and outlines the four phases of the equitable and social change process (ESCP). This process, which I have developed, guides equity leaders and social justice advocates through four phases of change and introspection starting with awareness. Chapter 5 focuses on awareness and advocacy of global educational issues affecting schools on a local and state level. Each issue discussed has implications for how students are treated justly and fairly or provided and denied opportunities to high-quality education.

Chapter 6 focuses on activism and allyship formed by critically aware equity leaders working collaboratively with their respective teams to engage in strategic actions for social change. Chapter 7 leads the reader through a discussion on accountability and offers a twenty-question protocol for equity auditing. The final chapter, chapter 8, ends with a commitment to practice, additional reflection questions relative to the ESCP, and a call to action that I delivered in a speech to future equity leaders.

PART I

Why this Book, and Why Now?

Shatter the System is a play on the idea that systems and structures in America are pervasive and continue to perpetuate division, invisibility, and racial discrimination. These systems and structures should be torn down and replaced with something new and different. But, first, imagine what it looks like to dismantle something. You take it apart piece by piece. Next, you might discard and heave those pieces onto a trash pile or a dump truck for removal. Then, you haul those dismantled pieces away to be recycled or destroyed.

You are left with a foundation—a foundation that once allowed a dysfunctional system to stand. But, as it relates to education, this is a foundation not built for historically underrepresented and marginalized individuals to prosper and find success without navigating numerous obstacles. With that image in mind, a different approach might be necessary to skillfully, humbly center and advance equity in our lives and our work.

In that vein, we might need to *shatter the system*, including the foundation, ask for forgiveness, acknowledge the rightful owners of the land, at least symbolically ask permission to build something new, something better, something sustainable, and something more equitable. Essentially, it might be time to shatter discriminatory, biased, and ineffective policies, practices, and processes instead of sheltering the status quo.

The educational system has suffered the consequences of institutional, racially motivated division, discrimination, incrimination, and racist acts and activities for a long time. As Dr. Eddie Glaude Jr. espoused on an MSNBC news program, "the intimacy of racism must be acknowledged." It is embedded within families and community dynamics. It is covert and overt and it is a constant snag on the fabric of the American experiment that has the potential to unravel parts, or all, of democracy. This is an unrealized fear, but scaling efforts to change how race affects systems can be corrected if the American public chooses to do so.

In addition to race and racism, the educational system has been the victim of defunding and underfunding. It has also been mismanaged, mishandled, and suffers from thanklessness. It has been a societal martyr, scapegoat, and has endured unimaginable violence against its members. Yet, the educational system has persisted in spite of all its faults, flaws, and failings.

It is still a system that must be corrected to ensure all of those who enter—all who are willing participants and hang on to the hope that it, the system, will provide opportunities, options, and outcomes for them. So, as this section offers a critique of recurring and challenging themes, I acknowledge how education has been and remains as a pathway for individuals to achieve success.

This shattering of the system acknowledges that while no individual should have to compromise their desires to create a more equitable world and community, there is a realization that even in a systematic redesign, not everyone will benefit from the system in the same way. While that may be true, race, socioeconomic circumstance, language, gender, gender identity, and any other related lived and loved experience should never be a disadvantage or advantage to accessing education and opportunity.

This idea is not an indictment of a person's racial or historical privilege. It is not an attack on a person or that individual's personhood. Instead, it is about understanding that each person is implicated in doing the work of equity until all of the remarkable human differences an individual possesses cease to marginalize, otherize, and tokenize them. Until that happens, the equity work continues.

Part I will focus on race, gender, and socioeconomic social conditioning. These social conditionings have persisted in determining how individuals engage in relationships and develop attitudes and behaviors. Moreover, many of the emerging trends make it difficult for those affected by these elements to overcome.

Specifically, part I of this book will focus on four areas:

- the social conditions and conditioning that affect education;
- terms and definitions;

- a framing to guide the equity leader's thinking, behavior, and actions; and
- a critique of the current and historical issues in education.

Equitable change is very personal. Each experience a person has can affect or drive how and why that individual will implicate themselves in making every effort to honor the dignity of others. At times it is because of a person's encounters with inequity, bias, discrimination, and other negative ideologies about their intersection that cause them to start the personal journey to equity. It can create space and a willingness to unpack and source their thinking and behavior toward others or why they might have encountered great adversity because of who they are, where they live, or whom they love.

Chapter 1

The Effects of Social Conditioning on Education

You cannot change what you are not insulted by.

—Bishop T. D. Jakes

Equity is a journey to respect and value our human experiences and differences by ensuring that all individuals can access their world without their experiences and differences becoming barriers and obstacles to their successes and growth. Equity realized means that a person's humanity is not on display but honored and exalted as their truth. It means that the systems designed for some individuals to achieve are redesigned for all people to access. Equity means that each person is responsible for their present moments and for a future that acknowledges the past. Equity means that every person within the system works collectively to create a different reality where opportunity and fair treatment are practiced, and not simply declared.

Throughout *Shatter the System*, the reader will be presented with various terms and concepts. The terms and concepts defined, explained, or introduced in this chapter will deepen the reader's understanding of information presented in future chapters. Before defining the terms, it is important to understand the social conditionings that birthed many of these terms into existence and why these terms are important for equity leadership and social justice advocacy.

Let us discuss three specific social conditions that have persisted throughout the history of America and American education. While there are, arguably, other social conditions, these three remain constant. First, let us look at what social conditioning means generally.

SOCIAL CONDITIONING

"Social conditioning is the process by which people of a certain society are trained to think, believe, feel, want, and react in a way that is approved by the society or the groups within it. There are many causes, dimensions, beliefs, programming, and barriers that are interwoven within social conditioning" (Chylewski, 2021).

The ecosystems that feed these conditions and the ideologies that create social conditioning and biases are instilled in an individual early on, sometimes even before birth. For example, women have experienced historical marginalization in this country. This marginalization of women is found in laws, policies, practices, and human rights. Women and young girls have been forced to fight for the right to vote, be leaders, have careers in male-dominated fields, and to control their bodies.

These biases and conditions promote placing another person in certain categories according to gender, race, socioeconomic status, and so forth. These conditions can also influence how power is imposed upon individuals and groups of people or how power is used to deprive people of the feeling that they belong. Finally, social conditioning and biases can affect how individuals are exposed to the world and their communities.

These concepts can also influence how an individual accesses and experiences opportunities within their communities, especially when they have internalized that some opportunities are not meant for them. They may believe that attempting to reach a certain level of achievement might result in potentially traumatic experiences and undue and inhumane difficulties.

For example, suppose a young Latino boy continues to hear messages about his inabilities. Conflated with his racial construction, he may begin to internalize those messages and forfeit his promise to another person because that person has been socially deemed as the rightful owner of the sought-after opportunity. Suppose a young Black girl is conditioned to believe that she should take on responsibilities that forfeit her childhood or has other people project more mature expectations onto her. In that case, she will perpetuate those ideological conditions through her behavior. It happens all too often. These examples highlight both power imposition and adultification, which will be defined and discussed later.

The structure upon which this country was built was very clear about who was eligible to hold positions of power and the role and rights of everyone else. This patriarchal structure led to systems that did not acknowledge women as equal and did not respect the humanity of people of color.

Those living in poverty were pushed into a marginalized working class of people with little to no education or access to resources. And when Jim Crow laws infected our nation, those divides, especially among poorer citizens, deepened. For some people, the intersectionality of multiple strains of social conditioning has created decades of multigenerational challenges and traumas.

While there are arguably other social conditions that have emerged over the last several centuries in America, three persist in dividing people and creating social and cultural tensions. We need only look throughout the halls of history to find movements, uprisings, laws, and policies aimed at bringing awareness to and correcting how these conditions have manifested in our lives. So let us examine these conditions in greater detail.

GENDER, IDENTITY, AND SOCIAL CONDITIONING

Without going too far back in history, women have struggled to gain equal rights with men in this country. Unfortunately, poor women, women of color, and those immigrating from other countries within the last few decades have experienced some of the worst social traumas and actions meant to maintain their social status and standing as inferior.

For example, it took an entire movement for some women to earn the right to vote through the Nineteenth Amendment. Women of color, who were afforded a loophole in an earlier amendment, continued to be blocked from exercising their constitutional right to access the voting booth, while their white counterparts could. Disallowing all women to vote continued to perpetuate marginalization and inhumanity. Thus, women of color had to continue to fight for their rights to vote and be fully and humanely recognized.

In the 1960s and throughout the 1970s, women led movements and called attention to equality, access to education, the right to control their bodies, and liberation from the patriarchal rule. Indeed, even before 1960, women, especially women of color, played significant roles in the civil rights movement. They marched and protested alongside men and demonstrated great strength and character in demanding fairness and equality.

In addition, many of these feminist movements laid a foundation for more modern-day gender equality and marriage equality movements. All of these movements, in essence, were calls for equity. These movements were also calls to redesign systems and structures of inequity or to eliminate barriers and obstacles, and discriminatory practices against underrepresented and marginalized groups.

Today, these issues persist and have greatly affected the educational system in many ways. There are increasingly discriminatory policies and practices that plant divisiveness, misinformation, and bias. Generations of students, if not careful, will continue to follow or deepen the divides modeled by the present and past generations of Americans.

Schools and educators are told by lawmakers what they can and cannot teach. Educators are also told by lawmakers how they should qualify or disqualify students' access to certain activities and programming based on their gender identity or orientation. Multiple debates are happening across the country related to race-and gender-conscious education.

Thinking about who belongs, what types of programming will be offered in certain schools and not in others, a deficit tax base and lack of funding for some schools and an overabundance of resources—financial and otherwise—for other schools, has created haves and have nots. To deepen the insult, many of these lawmakers exclude educators, those in the classrooms and working with students every day, from important conversations, thus making experiential and authentic teaching almost impossible.

These educators are bombarded with barriers and obstacles. Those who understand the need to redesign education and those who want to respect and value the humanity and dignity of their students are halted from doing so. Look no further than laws sweeping the country written to remove the teaching of a complete history and linking it to theories that most people are not exposed to until college and later in graduate school, like Critical Race Theory (CRT).

Other laws block students from participating in sports because of who they are and how they love. Fear and fear-mongering have infiltrated schools and classrooms, so much so that many teachers are leaving the profession they love. They are frustrated and demoralized, and many cite the constant attack on the profession as unconscionable and, in some instances, an abhorrent interference in teaching children how to think critically and examine the world in which they live.

Arguably, the laws are only one factor. Unfortunately, when you focus on education at the local level, school boards, parents, and sometimes the educators themselves engage in policies and practices that uphold the status quo, or create new policies and procedures in an attempt to control how students engage with one another. What is incredibly sad about this is that these individuals carry these ideologies into the schools and the classroom, where students then model the same divisive behaviors. Perhaps there needs to be a change in ideology and practices, and an increased focus on modeling humility and a branding of trust as an essential component of a thriving school system.

RACE AND SOCIAL CONDITIONING

Historic and common narratives about racial disparities typically focus on individual racism without recognizing or, more accurately, acknowledging the systemic and structural issues that maintain racialized inequities. This can be particularly troublesome when calls to remedy the egalitarian policies go unheard. For example, in a study conducted in 2009, researchers addressed the shift from ideological and individual prejudice and racist acts by bad actors, without addressing the systems in place that allow such acts to occur or those actors to operate (Brown et al., 2009).

These researchers argued there is a difference in how people engage in discrimination today than in our most recent past. It is more likely that discrimination or racial animus is characterized by projecting that people of color, particularly those who identify as Black or African American, violate American idealism related to work ethic, tradition, and impulsivity. They speculated how white people have been taught to believe that these idealized American constructs are genetically oriented and may lead some white people to think that Black people are somehow incapable of improving their lives.

Common messages perpetuated throughout history are that Black people and people of color, in general, are lazy, unintelligent (or possess inferior intelligence), violent, and dangerous. While these notions are untrue, such messages have been preserved throughout American society and imprinted into the country's social and cultural DNA. It is evident in the media, television, movies, news, and, unfortunately, in the educational system.

And in the educational system, these messages influence the type of curriculum students in predominantly minority schools can access, how they are disciplined, and the types of interventions and support provided. In addition, the idea that Black people are inferior and incapable is a deeply rooted belief that can be traced back to slavery. While this book does not delve deeply into that premise, historical framing is ever-present in our schools, classrooms, and communities.

Presently, movements and Black affinity messaging have been incorrectly branded as anti-patriotic, violent disobedience, and thwarting authority. Unfortunately, this branding eventually finds its way into schools and classrooms. As a result, schools are unknowingly put into a difficult position and are reluctant to ease policies that perpetuate discrimination and racial bias. Yet, at times, schools are perfectly positioned to end discriminatory policies and practices if their key people leverage their power and position.

Therefore, when the narrative is simply about individual racism, it is easier to point out bad actors, and for well-intentioned white people, in particular, to declare themselves antiracist. The problem is you cannot simply declare yourself antiracist and then default to the automatic responses that maintain the status quo. A person must recognize that the action taken to influence and change systems is not what is most difficult. It is the thinking about and willingness to unlearn and reflect on yourself and your practices that is challenging. Furthermore, people make the policies. So, suppose the people or person are/is unwilling to change, or find/s the mental effort to change uncomfortable and challenging. In that case, the system remains the same, and the inequities continue to oppress, marginalize, and otherize people.

When people focus too narrowly on individual racism, while it persists in America, focusing on it sharpens the scope on the so-called failings of people of color—the commonly communicated messages about patterns of behavior, poor choices, inferior work ethic, and other such disparate narratives (Spievack & Okeke, 2020). It also can have the opposite effect on burdening people of color with solving racism, which is neither their responsibility nor creation. So, again, shift the conversation from individual acts or bad actors to institutional oppression, bad actions, and discriminatory policies.

These messages have been imprinted in America's social and cultural DNA for so long that even people of color have internalized those messages about themselves and others within the same (or similar) sociocultural group. Additionally, when people focus on individual racist acts, sometimes the larger narrative is displaced.

As a result, you miss the opportunity to address systems of oppression and institutional racism, and you also miss the opportunity to engage in a fuller understanding and accounting of history. Moreover, when these global messages and insights are discounted, the robust individual narratives that can challenge biases and identify discriminatory practices and policies are discounted, policed, and lost.

The messages people have internalized about themselves and each other form another layer of social conditioning that is unfortunately influenced by racial construction and oppression. The challenge is unearthing the root cause of these messages to engage in efforts to interrupt, disrupt, and shift thinking and discussions from simply declaring someone as a racist or not, as a criminal or not, as a qualified candidate or not, and perhaps as a high-achieving student or not.

In addition to the broader description of this particular conditioning are the nuanced levels that address specific movements, affinity messages, and the intersection of social status, class, and race, and how these components have influenced education. For example, for several decades, race and poverty have been conflated.

A standard framing perpetuated about Black and brown people from low-earning, low-wealth households or who live in low-wealth communities is that they do not care about their children's education. This is simply untrue. Yet, again, this is a narrative that many educators have heard or have been taught, intentionally and unintentionally. Without understanding these families' full history, an individual defaults to their assumptions and biases and does not do the intentional work of shifting their thinking to influence their behavior and actions.

Anecdotes that are too often downloaded into the consciousness of teachers are "those kids" should not be expected to perform at a high enough level to meet standards, and "those other kids" who do are somehow exceptional, special, and a credit to their race. Now, these messages are not always overtly stated, but the sentiment is undoubtedly present.

These nuanced notions hinder and affect how teachers interact with particular students, the type of instruction offered to students, and how some students are disciplined and valued. These messages can also be found in the thinking of college faculty and leaders, and show up as people of color pursue their desired careers.

Students of color in institutions of higher education are sometimes labeled as "unprepared" and "not ready" to engage in scholarly work. Then, these students are often placed in remediation or transitional courses. Many students in these situations have secured student loans to afford college and those students use student loan funds to pay for these transitional courses, sometimes without receiving college credit while running up enormous amounts of student loan debt. Black students, for example, often have two to three times the student loan debt as their white peers (Education Data Initiative, 2021). This continues to widen the wealth gap, as many of these students of color have lower wage jobs, even with their college degrees.

Fortunately, some colleges and universities have recognized this as a serious and inequitable practice and have implemented concurrent credit courses and co-curricular programming to address this problem. They have also pushed for more funding and seek to provide more students of color with scholarships to afford college and leave with little to no student debt.

However, the more global issue is addressing and acknowledging that these students have done the best they can with, in some instances, an inferior K–12 education experience. Therefore, their seeming lack of preparedness or readiness for the demands of college is a much larger failure of the educational system itself.

Another related message that is often projected is that students of color have a shared experience simply because of the color of their skin. While there is certainly some natural skinship—a colloquial term for groups of people who share the same skin tone or a similar culture—not all experiences of students of color are the same.

The individual's story is not honored when this belief guides thinking and behavior. This is particularly the case in majority-minority schools with a white majority of teachers in the classroom. The following conversation between two teachers in the teachers' breakroom exemplifies how this typically unfolds and can cause harm and mistrust. This conversation also exemplifies how individuals are conditioned socially and culturally toward biases and coded narratives.

It's the first three weeks of school. Mr. Ramos is a new teacher and recent graduate. He knows the importance of building a culture for learning and is still working on cultivating a classroom culture where students feel valued. For the past few weeks, he's been struggling to find other creative ways to help his students to engage in conversation and trust that the classroom is a safe space. He is particularly concerned about one student's lack of engagement. A colleague suggested that he talk with Mrs. Hamilton.
"Mrs. Hamilton, do you have a minute to talk?"
"Sure, what's up?"
Mrs. Hamilton has taught at Ginsburg Middle School for the last eight years. Ginsburg's student population is 45 percent Black, 35 percent Latinx/Hispanic, and 20 percent identify as biracial or multiracial. Mrs. Hamilton is the most liked teacher by students. They find her easy to talk to and she challenges them to do their best. They like her "Real Talk" sessions after school and how she advocates for the students' needs and teaches them how to advocate for themselves.

The majority of the teachers at Ginsburg are teachers of color, 45 percent are Black, 25 percent are Latinx/Hispanic, and 30 percent are white.

Mr. Ramos continued, "So, I'm having some trouble with creating a culture where students feel like it's a safe space. I'm also having some trouble, particularly, with Jensen. She never wants to talk, share, or engage in conversation with me or her peers. She just doesn't seem to get it. I know kids from her circumstance can have some difficulties, but I know she has a lot to offer, and I would like to figure out the best way to help her. Plus, I really want my classroom to be a valued learning space where students can really talk."

In this scenario, Mr. Ramos makes assumptions about Jensen. His biased framing about who she is and what her circumstances are could potentially harm his ability to develop a rapport with her. This could also affect his desire for students to acknowledge his classroom as valued or safe. It is critical that Mr. Ramos continuously cultivates this safe and valued space that he desires for his students.

This racial, social, and cultural conditioning is not just a problem for Black or African American people. It is a problem for all Black, indigenous, people of color (BIPOC), and white people. This malign treatment of other human beings allows the system and structure to continue and sustain policies and practices that block others from accessing the fullness of their world because of their diversity. Therefore, a declaration of antiracism, for example, or standing in solidarity with a group of people or persons from an underrepresented or marginalized group is not enough without demonstrating a continuous and intentional commitment to change—to change a culture and remedy the wrongs.

SOCIOECONOMIC AND SOCIAL CONDITIONING

The final social condition cuts across race and gender. It is conflated with race and gender. The impact of wealth, income, class, and social standing is all related to the social conditioning of socioeconomics and education. In an article about the connection between the cultural and structural causes of poverty, Gregory Jordan (2004) found that the socioeconomic condition of people in poverty limits their perspectives on viable choices. Therefore, their behavior will serve as a proxy for social and cultural pathologies and reinforce harmful conditioning for future generations (Jordan, 2004). Thus, creating conditions for multigenerational trauma and sustainable wealth disparities to persist.

There is a common misconception that poverty results from the personal choices an individual or a group of individuals make. That is simply illogical. Arguably, no one who is poor or living in a low-wage community is making a personal choice to be in that situation. It is a daily struggle that many individuals face to access resources that might lift them out of their impoverished conditions. Poverty is a structural issue—an issue that has disproportionately affected people of color.

This misconception of personal choice and individual responsibility is a deeply rooted phenomenon in American culture. The idea that if someone is educated, works hard, follows all of the social, societal, and cultural rules, and adheres to the moral values framing American idealism they will be successful is not always the case. Often, those living in poverty have compounding and interrelated systemic and structural issues that compromise and contribute to their lack of access, upward mobility, and financial stability.

These interrelated structural and systemic disparities continue to grow divides instead of close gaps. For example, when a family is confronted with transportation, education, child care, health care, and affordable housing issues, it can affect the degree to which they believe they can ever progress and move closer to the American dream so many idealize.

When you add racial and gender disparities on top of these issues, it can be a crushing blow for those families, many finding a pathway out of poverty blocked. The social and cultural messages about who they are and who they will and can become are flawed and coded by biases, stereotypes, and internalized feelings of inadequacy. Again, the behaviors and actions can sometimes reflect the despair of poverty and the ever-present anger of oppression conditioning.

More abhorrently is how the criminal justice and school systems create a pipeline into prison for many students of color, especially, and some white students primarily in poorer rural communities. This pipeline is fostered through expulsion, suspension, truancy, and accepting that drop-out rates are expected in certain communities.

In a recent and explosive report by *ProPublica*, Black and Latinx children as young as eight were arrested and jailed for behaviors categorized as criminal acts—such as being a bystander or instigating a fight—that were neither criminal nor illegal. The judge overseeing these cases admitted to jailing children as young as seven and was reported to have said that jailing eight- and nine-year-old children was becoming a common practice. Many of these children entered into therapy as a result of experiencing such unimaginable trauma.

To be fair, some school officials and police officers were opposed to such treatment, yet these behaviors, practices, and policies continued for several years. As a result, these children's school experiences, beliefs about school, and sense of belongingness, values, and deservingness will forever be shrouded by a veil of inhumanity.

In closing, it is also vital to avoid characterizing the conflation of race and poverty and projecting that as the narrative for all people of color. That is another common misinterpretation and misconception and, frankly, the frustration of many BIPOC. Indeed, the stories are more varied and nuanced and speak to the richness of an individual's story and how they reflect who they are as a part of a larger social and cultural group.

Many people of color have found great success and achievement, and have gained access to opportunities through education and the workforce. However, there is a history of middle-class and upper-middle-class people of color whose stories and histories go untold and are viewed as exceptional. In some ways, these individuals have attained parts of the American Dream that have eluded others. The issue is these individuals and families are too often seen as exceptions and not the rule. Individuals who find themselves in the middle and upper classes often continue to contend with racial bias, stereotyping, tokenization, and othering.

The social conditioning discussed here is a part of the ongoing struggle to shift our thinking, actions, and behaviors toward centering and advancing equity. It starts with an understanding and exploration of "why." Then, as individuals and groups of people begin to unpack their why, they can progress toward making some determinations about how to leverage their power, positions, and privileges to effect change. Anything less is a failure to critique the system that you might benefit from and continue to perpetuate historical and demonstrative ideologies and institutional oppression.

In the next chapter, you will explore terms and definitions that will contextualize discussions in later chapters. Before moving on to chapter 2, think about the key chapter takeaways and use the reflection questions to engage in discussion with others or self-reflection and analysis.

The key chapter takeaways are:

- Social conditioning has greatly influenced how students are perceived and treated, and the quality level of education they are provided. These conditionings can also influence how students view themselves and their place in their schools and in larger society.
- Social conditioning is connected to policies, procedures, and practices within schools that directly affect students of color, girls,

those who identify as LGBTQIA+, students from low-wealth families, and under-resourced communities.
- The pervasiveness of social conditioning is deeply rooted. Acknowledging how conditioning has created (and continues to create) inequities is a first step in shifting the educational system for social change.

Reflection and Ideas to Consider

1. In what ways has the social conditioning discussed in this chapter affected your life and/or the lives of your family, friends, and neighbors? How might these social conditions have influenced your school or organizational setting?
2. What thoughts and insights were triggered after reading the scenario featuring Mr. Ramos and Mrs. Hamilton? If asked to intervene in the situation, what would be your response?
3. How have misperceptions, misconceptions, and misinformation about race, gender, identity, and socioeconomics played a part in the policies and practices within your local school community, and how have those in positions of power to responded to affect change?

SELECTED REFERENCES

Brown, T., Akiyama, M., White, I., Jayaratne, T., & Anderson, E. (2009). Differentiating contemporary racial prejudice from old-fashioned racial prejudice. *Race Social Problem, 1*(2): 97–110.

Chylewski, K. (2021, March 10). Has social conditioning been holding women back from leadership roles? *BetterUp*. https://www.betterup.com/blog/has-social-conditioning-been-holding-women-back-from-leadership-roles.

Romano, A. (2020, October 9). A history of wokeness. *Vox*. https://www.vox.com/culture/21437879/stay-woke-wokeness-history-origin-evolution-controversy.

Schein, E., & Schein, P. (2018). *Humble leadership: The power of relationships, openness, and trust.* Oakland, CA: Berrett-Koehler Publishers.

Spievack, N., & Okeke, C. (2020, February 26). How we should talk about racial disparities. *Urban Wire* (the blog of the Urban Institute). https://www.urban.org/urban-wire/how-we-should-talk-about-racial-disparities.

Chapter 2

Definitions and Terms

The secret of education lies in respecting the pupil.

—Ralph Waldo Emerson

There are many terms, concepts, movements, and theories discussed throughout this book. Chapter 2 will define and discuss those items in detail to ensure an accurate context and enrich your understanding. Many of the terms are commonly used, but for this book, these terms are presented in a nuanced context. Some of these terms have rich and storied histories.

Other terms presented in this chapter are current and trending, and are used to explain different cultural ideologies. The definitions, descriptions, and scopes of these terms will shed light on their historical, current, shifting, and emerging understandings.

adultification. A form of bias where children of color, in particular, are treated as adults. The expectations and typical child development are prematurely advanced. This term is often synonymous with the ways in which children of color are expected to handle predominantly adult events and responsibilities. These children might be exposed to more adult language and themes. As a result, their behaviors and actions might appear more adult-like, and they may imitate adult behaviors without enough developmental understanding of the behaviors they are imitating.

Adultification can come in many forms. However, Black girls seem to be overwhelmingly affected. This has been a growing problem in schools where their behavior is deemed inappropriate and where teachers and other school personnel misplace expectations of their behavior. This is often a factor in the rise in suspension and expulsion rate of Black girls and other girls of color.

allyship. A group of people engaged in active and consistent leveraging of power and privilege to address the needs of marginalized communities to ensure equity is realized. Self-identification of those who declare themselves an ally should be held to account for how they demonstrate their allyship. Their actions should not be performative or promote a person's ally resume but, rather, transformational and influential.

One of the most critical points in creating an allyship with a marginalized group or person is to understand their story and how an individual can leverage their power and privilege and build trust with that group. Another critical factor is to understand oneself and examine and understand privilege in relation to others—not apologize for it or feel bad because of it, but use it to advance equity.

Blackness. A cultural and social belonging phenomenon associated with those of the Black and African diaspora. It is related to race, but it is more appropriately defined by expressions of the culture within the racial group. Blackness can inform others of an individual's lived experiences and can nuance the implication of class, wealth, skin tone, affinity messaging, and gender.

Blackness is often used to counter the societal and historical messages of whiteness as superior and aspirational. Movements, affinity messaging, organizations, and institutions (i.e., Black Lives Matter, Black excellence, historically Black colleges and universities, etc.) have attempted to change how Black people across the diaspora are treated and viewed differently within and outside of the culture.

cancel culture. A social media phenomenon that started within various platforms where individuals withdraw their support of a person, usually a group, business, or organization that declares, expresses, or behaves in a way that is counter to another person's beliefs, values, and/or ideologies. It is most often projected onto those with highly visible political, public, and social profiles.

Cancel culture comes under great scrutiny and has become a political talking point. Some are proponents of canceling a person figuratively or canceling their support of a person when they say or do something egregious that causes harm, or does not hold to strict normalization of the purity of a role model, or engages in a behavior or action, or says something that is counter to their perceived brand.

Cancel culture has transgressed and ended the careers of some individuals in the public eye. In education, cancel culture has damaged the reputation of teachers, students, families, and other school personnel and has become such a rigid phenomenon that it does not allow for mistakes or their correction.

coded narrative. An accounting of events and attributes that an individual projects onto another person based on personal experiences, interactions, social and cultural conditioning, and biases. The stereotypes, biases, and personal experiences of an individual are projected onto someone else.

These elements combine to create a narrative that is not authentic to one individual but is created by another. These coded narratives are typically influential in how a person interacts and builds relationships with others. The idea is borrowed from the coding industry in that the code that is projected is created by someone else and therefore carries a great deal of bias. It is antithetical to the power of the authentic narrative.

Critical Race Theory. A theory that promotes an examination of how race impacts the policies, practices, and processes within a system or structure. The theory was introduced by Kimberlé Crenshaw and others decades ago and has most often been taught in graduate school and, more specifically, in law school. Over the years, the theory has evolved to include more identity intersections and the role race plays in those areas.

de-biasing. A strategy that promotes the use of cultural humility, civility, and compassion to shift an individual's behavior and actions toward creating a more equitable environment. Micro-affirmations and high-engagement techniques are often used when one is de-biasing.

de-coupling. A strategy that promotes a shift in thinking to challenge beliefs, values, and ideologies that discriminate, negate, and dishonor another person's being. From an organizational level, it is engaging the remediation and correction of, and the accountability for, any systemic inequity. Thus, the strategy is inextricably aligned to de-biasing.

ethos. The cultural spirit of a workplace guided by its members' thoughts, behaviors, and actions. The ethos allows equity to advance and root itself within a sustainable and accessible environment and atmosphere.

equity auditing. A process that evaluates the degree to which systemic and structural corrective actions are implemented.

equity leader(ship). A person who guides the strategic actions and visioning through humility, compassion, and belongingness. Humility, which is discussed later in the equity framing section, speaks to how we capitalize and engage freedoms of judgment and biases. Compassion in this context is described by a person's ability to learn about and understand the narratives of others, and to use their power and privileges to create or influence change.

equity roadmap. A process that creates benchmarks and mile markers of progress and success in centering and advancing equity. The roadmap directs the organization's path and is directly aligned to an organization's mission and vision. At each mile marker, the organization or group should assess progress, propose changes, when necessary, and evidence work. The roadmap also includes how the individuals within the group or organization center fairness, justice, diversity, and inclusiveness. The roadmap is intertwined with strategic equity planning.

historically/traditionally underrepresented and marginalized groups. These terms typically referred to people of color, LGBTQIA+ individuals, sometimes women. These are individuals and groups who have been historically discriminated against, endured systemic and structural oppression, and have led many movements and shifts in how society treats, respects, and honors the constitutional rights of citizens.

These groups, particularly people of color and those individuals who identify as LGBTQIA+, have experienced some of the most significant systemic atrocities.

individual racism. Individual actors pursuing and engaging in discriminatory, biased, harmful, and, sometimes, violent acts against others, particularly those of marginalized and underrepresented groups.

institutional racism. The ideologies, thinking, and actions that perpetuate and sustain systemic and structural oppression and discrimination. This type of racism has matured over time and has maintained the status quo or created policies, laws, and actions. What is most dangerous about institutional racism is the way in which the so-called mainstream and the marginalized have normalized the behaviors.

intersectionality. The way in which a person's identities overlap to tell an authentic story of who that person is through their experiences, emotionality, and evidence.

marginalized. An individual or group of people who have been historically excluded, mistreated, and their voices and personhood dismissed. This marginalization is often perpetuated by the dominant culture—also known as majority culture—against others based on various categories of diversity and representation.

otherizing. An incredibly harmful practice most closely aligned to marginalizing. However, it is often associated with identifying people, and especially people of color as a different class of people. The term capitalizes on a person's difference to project diversity.

oppression. Is when a social group in power dehumanizes other social groups and keeps them in that state (Freire, 1970). Psychological oppression is social oppression that requires systems and structures to maintain the oppressive ideologies and thrives on the internal subjugation by the oppressed person (Hanson, 2021). Oppression is manifested in four different ways: primary, secondary, tertiary, and mixed (Hanna, Talley, & Guindon, 2000).

privilege. Social, ideological, cultural, and sometimes invisible rights, benefits, and advantages that individuals and groups hold over other individuals and groups of people.

power. Unequal influence over the distribution and access to resources, including education, wealth, and citizenship. It is also characterized by a collective strength within a group and is relational. It is controlled and wielded by one group of people over another.

power imposition. A practice of promoting and offering access to resources, information, programs, and so on, based on biases about and the discrimination of certain groups of people (Sue, 2016). It is related to unconscious and conscious bias and institutional oppression and racism. In schools, power imposition and deprecation, defined next, are highly prevalent.

It fosters the way in which students are funneled into and encouraged to participate in particular sports. It promotes how students are encouraged to seek advanced placement (AP) courses and gift and talented (GT) classes. It might affect the expulsion and suspension of retained students. Imposition and deprecation also affect how policies, standards, and expectations are levied for students.

power deprivation. A practice of exclusion and not offering access to resources, programs, and information based upon unconscious and conscious biases and discrimination and institutional racism and oppression.

protectionism. Holding beliefs, values, and privileges in the highest esteem and not creating space to acknowledge other people's perspectives or new learning that challenges one's thinking. This is especially dangerous and harmful when the thinking is protected, even when illogical or causes hurt to others and self. It can also negatively affect someone's ability to learn more about how other people represent their humanity.

social justice advocacy. A process or state of raising the awareness of, defending, or promoting the interest of a group, primarily related to human rights, systemic and structural issues, and the experiences of oppressed, marginalized, or underrepresented groups of people.

social justice activism. Organized advocacy efforts to affect and influence policies, practices, thinking, and laws to remedy inequities and protect the human rights of marginalized and underrepresented groups of people.

strategic equity planning. A process of creating a document or plan that focuses on meaningful accountable and strategic actions and outcomes. It is characterized by a determinative mission, vision, results, and an ethos to support the plan. Strategic equity planning moves groups from a performative effort to meaningful and accountable actions.

tokenization. The selection of a person based on an obvious or articulated difference to reflect desired idealized qualities of a majority or dominant culture. It is sometimes considered covert racism because it gives white people the appearance of being non-racist and supportive of diversity. Typically, the person who is tokenized is burdened with the responsibility of representing an entire culture, race, or social group that is largely oppressed and/or recognizes they are being used as a prop.

woke/wokeness. A colloquial term that began in communities of color as early as the 1920s. The term was firmly rooted in the cultural consciousness of present-day generations of people of color after the murder of Michael Brown in 2014. The term gained sociopolitical capital and was co-opted outside of communities of color and infused into the mainstream consciousness. The original meaning was a call for people of color, particularly Black people, to become socially conscious and aware.

It became a rallying cry for the Black Lives Matter movement and other race- and gender-conscious movements and was reintroduced through social media, music, and movies. Throughout the years, the term has generally maintained its original content. However, like many Black vernacular phrases, to "stay woke" has become a polarizing phrase. It is also used as a counter-message to cancel culture. In 2020, *Vox* published an interesting report on the history of woke, wokeness as a "watchword" for spotlighting deception and social and racial animus (Romano, 2020).

valued-conversational space. Is a space where individuals feel confident in contributing their ideas and perspectives, and engaging in a dialogue and conversation. The conversational space is not declarative but a commitment to cultivating respect and honoring the dignity of others.

whiteness/white identity. According to *The National Museum of African American History and Culture*, whiteness refers to how white people—their customs, culture, and beliefs—operate as the standard against which all other groups are compared. Whiteness is also at the core of understanding race in America. Whiteness, and the normalization of white racial identity, throughout America's history has created a culture where nonwhite persons are seen as inferior or abnormal.

In closing, the definitions and terms presented in this chapter will be revisited in subsequent chapters to add context to the content discussed in those chapters. Below are a few questions and ideas to consider using with your team or for self-reflection. In the next chapter, I will discuss equity leaders, leadership, and social justice advocates. Core values for those roles will be defined and how these roles can be effective by first outlining a commitment to examine oneself and acknowledging the interpersonal skills required for equity work to be sustainable.

The key chapter takeaways are:

- Defining and understanding the origins of cultural terms that are current and trending allows for richer conversations and helps to add clarity to cultural phenomena.
- Engaging in a discussion of terms, theories, and concepts can help the equity leader or the social justice advocate define their role. A discussion of terms can also help them implicate other people in deepening their awareness and understanding and engage in operationalizing equity in their respective work settings.

Reflection and Ideas to Consider

1. How would you use these definitions and descriptions in your work and within your circle of influence?
2. Have these terms and definitions added to your understanding? What particular term, theory, or definition has primed you to want to know more?
3. If you were to create a valued conversational space, as defined above, how would you explain the difference between advocacy and activism and what would you diagnose as an issue of equity to challenge and correct?

REFERENCES

Freire, Paulo (1971) [1970]. *Pedagogy of the oppressed*. Translated by Ramos, Myra Bergman. New York: Herder and Herder. OCLC 1036794065.

Hanna, F., Talley, W., & Guindon, M. (2000). The power of perception: Toward a model of cultural oppression and liberation. *Journal of Counseling and Development* (78), 430–441.

Hanson, M. (2021). Student loan debt by race. Center for Cultural Research Education Data Initiative. https://educationdata.org/student-loan-debt-by-race.

Romano, A. (2020, October 9). A history of wokeness. *Vox*. https://www.vox.com/culture/21437879/stay-woke-wokeness-history-origin-evolution-controversy.

Sue, D. (2016). *Race talk and the conspiracy of silence: Understanding and facilitating difficult conversations about race*. Hoboken, NJ: Wiley Publishing.

Chapter 3

Equity Leadership and Social Justice Advocacy

We need to make equity and justice a priority today and every day.

—Candice Dowd Maxwell

Equitable change is a personal process that requires a person to make a concerted and continuous effort to think differently and behave differently. It also requires a certain level of courage to face adversity, nay-sayers, and those who will protect the status quo and their comfortable positions of power. This type of committed activism begins with understanding your role as an equity leader and setting the advocacy wheels in motion for change.

In this chapter, I will:

- revisit definitions and expand your thinking about engaging in and leading substantive equity efforts;
- make a case for acknowledging the impact of personal experiences and relationships and how those experiences guide why someone might implicate themselves in doing the work;
- discuss how the leader should always make every effort to honor the dignity of others and advocate for specific needs with broader implications; and
- expose the importance of navigating the system to interrupt the status quo and effect necessary change.

This Trojan horse type of approach has tremendous implications for individuals and groups engaging in equity efforts and corrective actions. However, first, let us revisit what equity leadership is and how equity leaders can also be social justice advocates.

EQUITY LEADERS, LEADERSHIP, AND SOCIAL JUSTICE ADVOCATES

An equity leader is someone who guides strategic and equitable actions through humility, compassion, and belongingness. This individual understands their role is to influence other people's thinking through awareness and lead efforts to undo hardened discriminatory policies and highlight practices that might discriminate against other people and protect the status quo.

An equity leader recognizes the power of the authentic narrative and honors the personal journey of individuals as they grapple with their own biases and perhaps the source of those biases. Finally, and from an organizational perspective, an equity leader is committed to moving from awareness to accountability and corrective action and is ready to engage in difficult conversations about the complexities of equity issues.

A social justice advocate is someone who commits to an equitable change process and inclusive action. They are focused on raising awareness and/or defending the cause of a group—particularly a marginalized or underrepresented group of people. They might be intricately involved in human rights, correcting systemic and structural issues, and acknowledging the experiences of oppressed, marginalized, or underrepresented groups of people.

Equity work often falls to a few people committed to it, while others might have simply proclaimed their solidarity for a group about a particular problem or experience. In this instance, the individual is primed to challenge long-standing and long-held systemic beliefs, practices, and policies that disadvantage other people, mainly if those discriminatory practices and beliefs are based on race, gender, identity, religion, or ability. The social justice advocate is generally concerned about and can engage others in strategic conversations and planning to act responsively for other people's needs and issues.

Equity leaders and advocates can be one in the same person, or an individual positioned to build an allyship of other concerned individuals to begin the process of *equity road mapping*. This process creates benchmarks and mile markers of progress and success in centering and advancing equity.

The roadmap directs the organization's path and is directly aligned to an organization's mission and vision. At each mile marker, the organization or group should assess progress, propose changes, when necessary, and evidence the work and equity efforts. The roadmap also includes how the group or organization centers fairness, justice, diversity, and inclusiveness. The equity roadmap is intertwined with strategic equity planning and can help communicate the mission and vision of the organization or group.

Equity Leadership Values and Competencies

There are generally four core values and competencies of an equity leader that allow this type of individual to be a competent social justice advocate in many ways. Indeed, other values and competencies may be necessary for an equity leader or social justice advocate in your school or organization. However, these four values are foundational for a model equity leader.

- *Humility.* Humility will be discussed in detail in a later chapter. For now, humility addresses how an individual demonstrates and engages freedom from judgment and bias and harmful or hurtful comments about others. This requires consistent reflection and a deep understanding of how the trifecta of power, position, and privilege compounds progress toward equitable outcomes and supports conformity or normalizing the status quo.

It is also necessary that the equity leader recognize the importance of self-discovery, pruning biased beliefs, being vulnerable and transparent, and being a seeker of knowledge. Moreover, when and if the leader has to engage in a difficult conversation, they may be better prepared because they have established rapport and can build authentic relationships with those they lead.

- *Compassion.* In this context, compassion is described by a person's ability to demonstrate understanding, learning, and acknowledgment of the authentic narratives of others, and the confirmation of their power and privilege to create social change. The compassionate, equity leader projects *micro-affirmation* into conversations, learns from the authentic narratives shared by others, and pushes other individuals to confront their unknowing and misinformation in a kind but direct manner.

Micro-affirmations are the subtle messages, statements, and comments that drive openness, trust, and respect. These messages are generally warm, inviting, respectful ways to communicate to other people that their voices matter and their insights are valued. These statements and messages are the direct opposite of microaggressions that typically are devaluing messages that marginalized individuals encounter frequently.

Microaggressions are so common that many people engage in this deficit language unconsciously. It is only when someone who has experienced these types of aggressions repeatedly brings the harm and hurt to the individual's attention does that person even recognizes the harm they may have caused. For many marginalized people, the weight of these constant interactions and experiences feels too often like a burden—a burden of carrying the hurt of insensitivities related to their identities and lived and loved experiences.

Micro-affirmations, when offered genuinely and consistently, become an effortless and normal way in which the equity leader, and really anyone, can create a sense of belonging within a group. These messages can also help to support a valued conversational space where equitable decisions and ideas can emerge and evolve. Review the box below for examples of micro-affirmations

To be compassionate in working on social justice issues and educating individuals around social justice is possible when those folks are engaged and implicate themselves in doing the work. However, they first have to be led into walking a personal path toward equity and unpacking the truth about the system or systems of which they are a part. This level of guidance is not easy but it is crucial to the process.

EXAMPLES OF MICRO-AFFIRMATION

"I would like your opinion on . . . "
"Have we missed anything critical to the discussion?"
"Let's have lunch tomorrow."
"Let's support small businesses of color for gift giving this year."
"Have we considered offering more extracurricular activities like . . . ?"
"Let's organize a college and apprenticeship tour for our middle schoolers."
"How can we expand on your ideas?"
"I appreciate you sharing your story with me."
"When could you share your ideas with leadership?'
"This is a good plan. Let's see what we can do to support it."
"Let's find some resources to help you move forward."
"How can I learn more about what you presented?"

- *Responsive decision-making.* In the role of an equity leader, a person has to be prepared to make the necessary decisions to ensure those in historically and traditionally marginalized groups gain access to opportunities and resources. For example, the leader may need to help others build skills and share their feelings and stories. The decisions should be grounded in a fundamental belief system that every person's narrative, history, background, and experiences should be acknowledged and heard. This allows belonging to flourish where valued conversations can lead to inclusive actions.

- *Capacity-building and collaboration.* Equity work is done best in partnership with other people. Why? Everyone has information to share and an experience with equity or inequity. Sharing these experiences can advance a deeper appreciation of someone's narrative and can be a clarion call to honor the dignity of their humanity.

Additionally, many people hold positions of power, and most individuals carry privileges that can be leveraged to help someone else access opportunities and resources. When a person and a group of people are working to build the capacity for cross-cultural alliances and partnerships, it is critical to identify what those privileges are of those in positions of power so that you can determine how best to leverage those privileges for others.

Therefore, working with other people helps people to implicate themselves in doing the work. They are more likely to recognize the value added by engaging in equity, and those individuals may make significant investments of time, energy, and resources to address inequities.

Equity leadership and social justice advocacy is characterized by a person's ability to build relationships, coalitions, and cross-cultural alliances to bring awareness to, interrupt, dismantle, and even shatter a system to create something better—a better and more equitable system or process. Leading in this manner is adaptive and distributive, and it should be.

The work becomes branded to the organization and not necessarily an individual. The work is also predicated on the involvement and commitment of other like-minded individuals—other individuals who are willing to confront the callousness of oppression and discrimination that may be present within their organizations. Therefore, the equity efforts are distributed among the group and the level of group interdependence allows for a greater sense of buy-in and accountability.

Furthermore, the work is adaptive. Meaning that the group works to diagnose the issue and redesign or engage in an equitable change process. This is all done with the goal of challenging the status quo. This is particularly true for schools that are expected to provide a quality and equitable learning environment for all students. All stakeholders are on deck, to use a baseball term, to shift the decades-long—centuries-long—practices in education and schools.

When an organization is involved in equity work, it is incumbent upon each person to understand their role and responsibility to shift their thinking. They must be willing to unpack their own biases and habits of thinking about others, especially if their thinking creates obstacles or barriers intentionally or unconsciously.

This commitment to reflective thinking or slow thinking, which will be discussed later in this chapter, allows for those individuals to engage in a deeper understanding of the historical and structural ideologies that are often deeply embedded in systems, making it difficult for those of particular marginalized and underrepresented groups to overcome.

Additionally, this type of personal response creates the condition for prolonged, forward progress and corrective action and accountability to frame a new and better system free of race, identity, and wealth-conscious disadvantages. A goal for educational equity leaders is to acknowledge the ideologies that plague the institution—that affect individuals' interpersonal relationships and the message people internalize about themselves and others. All of which works best when a person has navigated a system to dismantle it and rebuild it from within. This, the Trojan horse approach, is what I referred to earlier in this chapter and will be discussing in greater detail in the next section.

THE TROJAN HORSE APPROACH

Most people know the story of how the city of Troy was taken by the Greek soldiers who hid in a giant horse, which was thought to be a gift, and was brought into the city of Troy. Using that story as a metaphor, *shattering the system* will take someone or a group of people willing to identify the inequities within the educational system.

These educators are a part of the system that has historically disadvantaged others, and therefore, they are the people who can correct and change the system if they choose to critique the system that they may have also benefited from. In keeping with the Trojan horse analogy, it is the unwillingness of the person or people to act that can be the Achilles' heel to corrective change.

In education, teachers, leaders, counselors, parents, para-professionals, school board members, district leaders, lawmakers, lobbyists, professional associations, concerned community members, and even students are implicated in identifying inequitable issues and addressing or correcting those issues. Moreover, it is this coalition of people who are well positioned to ensure the changes are sustainable and grounded in the mission and vision of schools, and obstacles and barriers are eliminated.

A reformed education system is transformed through the stories, voices, and experiences of those who have been advantaged and disadvantaged. The school is transformed by the corrective action to policies and practices that govern how students learn and are treated with dignity. It is also transformed through legislation at the local, state, and federal levels. In addition, while broader federal systemic changes might seem unreachable, what is actionable are sweeping and sustainable changes at the state, local, and school levels.

What is tolerated in schools and how legislation is enacted across states will influence how students are treated, respected, educated, and supported in those schools. It is no secret that schools are not equal and the inequity of resources, access, and opportunity is baked into school systems. So, those school stakeholders who are working within the system have an obligation to be critical of the system and respond with a sense of urgency to make the necessary changes. Let us look at the following scenario to highlight a well-established and unaddressed issue related to advanced placement courses.

Ginsburg Middle School is in a racially and culturally diverse community. The school offers AP classes in English and math. The leadership team has disaggregated the last three years of data to address the issue of recruitment and placement of students of color in AP classes compared to their white counterparts. What they learn is that while students of color (Black and Latinx) make up 35 percent of the school's population, less than 3 percent of those students are in AP classes. While white students, who make up 50 percent of the student body, are disproportionately (37 percent) overrepresented in AP classes in comparison.

The team also noticed that 3 percent of the student population identifies as Native American. Yet, none of those students are in AP classes, and those who identify as Asian American are all in AP math. This is of great concern, and the team wants to look deeper into why this is happening and what they might do to shift thinking and increase the number of students of color in AP classes.

In this scenario, students of color are overwhelmingly underrepresented in AP classes, even though they make up 35 percent of the school population. This scenario is all too familiar and reflects the current state of affairs related to the gross underrepresentation of students of color in advanced coursework. This has been an issue of equity for decades in American schools. Moreover, denying, in many instances, students of color access to advanced coursework perpetuates negative messages about belonging and inclusion. It also sends a message about who should and should not be in advanced placement courses.

This type of unconscious ideology fuels *position imposition*—the practice of promoting and offering access to resources, information, programs, and so on, based on biases and discrimination against certain groups of people. It also supports *position deprivation*—a practice of exclusion and failing to offer access to resources, programs, and information based upon unconscious and conscious biases, discrimination, institutional racism, and oppression.

Typically, there are several arguments presented as to why students of color, in particular, are not promoted to AP coursework. Some of the commonly exposed arguments are presented in Table 3.1 along with the impact of those statements and arguments and how those messages are internalized.

The school's stakeholders are obligated and primed to address what the data has revealed about the inequities found within the recruitment, selection, and preparation of all students to seek advanced placement. A recent report indicates that in racially diverse schools, Black and Latinx students comprise less than 10 percent of students in AP courses. In fact, the inequities start in elementary school where many of this same group of students are not placed in gifted and talented programs.

In majority-minority schools, AP courses are less likely to even be offered as a part of the school's curriculum. What that says is that regardless of the racial make-up of the school students of color, specifically, Black and Latinx students are less like to find a pathway for advanced coursework. This ultimate message is you do not belong here nor will the option or opportunity be provided to you. It is classic power deprivation and imposition.

Table 3.1

Source: Author-created

Common Statements	Internalized Messages
These students are not prepared or ready for the rigor of AP classes.	These students are not intelligent enough to keep up with the high expectations of AP classes.
These classes are for those students who show great promise and are planning to attend college.	With the exception of a few, we are not optimistic that these students will do well in college, nor do we expect many of them to pursue college.
We see something special in students who are in AP classes.	AP classes are not an opportunity meant for everyone.
It will require a lot of parental support and supervision.	Those parents will not support their child's education.
Not all students have the aptitude for AP classes.	It is a selective process and for certain students.

Certainly, not all students will want to pursue advanced placement courses, but they should be prepared for the work and presented with the choice to pursue AP courses. What is most alarming about the lack of access to gifted and talented and AP programming is when students of color, and in this instance, Black and Latinx students are placed in gifted and talented and AP programming, they are overwhelmingly successful.

Therefore, the school and these stakeholders can shift and change the policies, practices, recruitment, selection, and preparation of their students with the goal of increasing the students of color who enroll in AP classes and gifted and talented programs. That is the Trojan horse approach. These educators are in the system. They are the Greeks who invaded Troy. They, the educators, only need to act to create change and not allow their unwillingness to challenge the status quo to continue to be the Achilles' heel that fails their students and perpetuates bias.

Advanced placement and gifted and talented are just one area where educational inequities are present. Bias and power imposition and deprivation are also apparent in sports, more specifically the type of sports offered in certain schools. For some schools, students have access to explore all sorts of interests including lacrosse, swimming and diving, golf, and other types of sports that often carry a certain elitist quality. While in other schools, students may have the option of playing football or basketball, track and field, and maybe baseball.

We might also see power imposition and deprivation play out in terms of who is encouraged to pursue band as opposed to orchestra, or who is encouraged to pursue the debate and speech team, and who is not represented. Some of the necessary changes will happen when individuals unpack their thoughts and approaches to education and educational attainment differently. In this instance, an equity leader also has to be an effective thought leader and attempt to shift their own and other people's responses from simply knowing to action. This next section will explore the shift from knowing to acting more deeply.

SHIFTING FROM THE AUTOMATIC RESPONSE TO REFLECTIVE RESPONSES

In Daniel Kahneman's book *Thinking, Fast and Slow* (2001), he suggests how a person thinks, behaves, and acts is a part of that individual's automatic thinking and response. Their unconscious thoughts and instincts guide their behavior. Moreover, their thinking and behaving have essentially been practiced countless times to the point of becoming automatic ways of being.

It is, then, through these automatic responses that a person will continue to interact and engage with others because those behaviors have simply been normalized. However, the goal for an equity leader and social justice advocate is to normalize a different habit of thinking and behaving so that a person's actions will align to more equitable thoughts—thoughts about how we treat, support, and serve others, and especially the marginalized. This means that these individuals will need to activate their reflective thinking.

Reflective thinking is characterized by conscious thoughts, intentions, and logic. It is a slower way of thinking, understanding, and processing information, new habits, and new ways of engaging with others in many ways. Think about this: many people in their forties drive on a daily basis. Most of those people have been driving for so long that the mechanics, the rules of the road, are just a part of their automatic response.

They essentially have hours and hours of practice. It is their automatic response. They simply have been driving the same way for a very long time and have normalized their driving behaviors. Some have normalized their behaviors so much so that they might feel as though they activated the autopilot or the self-driving mechanism even when those devices do not exist in their vehicles.

Think about what these same individuals have to consider in order to teach someone else how to drive. They now have to engage a slower part of their thinking to recall details, the specific sequence to starting a car, how much gas to give when accelerating, where the mechanics are in the car, what the indicator lights mean, and so on. It is an ordeal.

This is why parents of first-time drivers are extremely nervous and teaching a teenager how to drive is incredibly stressful. Some will leave it up to an expert or a more patient driving instructor. The point is that they, the driver, will have to engage their reflective thinking—*reflective response*, which is slower, more deliberate, and intentional. So how does this relate to an equity leader and social justice advocate?

A large part of the work is to influence others and provide new information or new perspectives that might not have been considered or recognized before. An equity leader can encourage or motivate others to think slowly—to reflect and not just engage in upholding or protecting the status quo. The leader or advocate can promote a willingness to engage in acknowledging the experiences of others and see and empathize with those experiences and slowly shift a person's thinking about the issue of equity or the way in which a person has been oppressed or disadvantaged by a system. It takes time, trust, openness, and a willingness to be vulnerable and determined.

Additionally, working for equity is ongoing. It is not a singular event and requires constant vigilance to move equitable thinking from a reflective response to automatic responses and the way in which an individual views the world. Specifically, the way an equity leader and social justice advocate shifts the mindset of school stakeholders to implement the necessary changes to ensure an equitable education is reachable and obtainable for all students is an example of moving from knowing what is wrong to doing something to change the conditions that have created the "wrong" to persist.

To be an effective and influential equity leader, it is critical to engage cultural humility, constantly reflect on and prune your own ideologies, and honor the interpersonal accountability needed to be a transformative leader for equity. This is a large part of the vulnerability that is important in this work because to be vulnerable means that you are being human.

You are exposing and examining your biases, assumptions, and identities. It is such a significant part that will help to explain and define the historical privileges, position, and power that a person might hold and how those elements inform how they operate within a system.

For an equity leader to be effective, they must engage in this ongoing work. This critical examination is a necessary function of the interpersonal work of an equity leader, social justice advocate, and individuals as a part of an allyship or coalition.

This pruning and exploration will aid the individual in avoiding the risk of reproducing systemic inequities within the historical structures that have centuries-long histories of alienating and locking students out of educational opportunities that should be available to all, especially in public schools.

As was said at the beginning of this chapter, equity leadership is a personal journey of reflection and the leader must be willing to not only declare equity as a driving force but also demonstrate how equity is internalized and embedded in their personal beliefs and exemplified through their work.

In the scenario presented above about Ginsburg Middle School, by engaging in slow, reflective thinking, the team can devise a different plan and process—a more equitable process to ensure that students have access to advanced placement to ensure fair representation.

They first need to examine themselves and how they operate within their school. Then they need to unpack and examine the policies, practices, and decisions about AP coursework. The next step might be to eliminate the barriers, redesign or rewrite policies that are blocking students from accessing AP courses, and then to engage in continuous monitoring of the new changes and hold all stakeholders accountable for ensuring the changes occur and without replacing one inequitable practice with another.

In closing, this chapter has defined equity leaders and social justice advocates and has provided some values and competencies of these roles. These values and competencies help to create a frame or a model by which an individual can measure their readiness and preparedness to lead equity efforts. Humility, compassion, capacity-building, and responsive decision-making are core values, yes, and support the need for the equity leader to be vulnerable and exercise cultural humility in order to engage in self-examination and openness to understanding the intersectionality of another person's identities and their narrative.

I have also shared some examples of how inequities are normalized practices, policies, and ways of thinking and behaving in school. It is certainly up to those individuals with the system, in this case, the educational or school system to create the changes necessary. Reflect on the questions below and the key takeaways to generate more ideas about how an equity leader and social justice advocate could help shift your organization or school's equity efforts. Think about the people in your school who are well positioned or open to taking on this type of role and work.

In the next chapter, a framework for the equity leader and social justice advocate will be discussed and defined. This framework is designed to provide a foundation for the transforming thinking, behaviors, and actions of individuals and organizations. This framing—humility, diversity, inclusion, and equity (HDEI)—adds value to how the equity leader or social justice advocate critiques their personal biases and constructs allyships and alliances to influence social change.

The key chapter takeaways are:

- The role of the equity leader and the social justice advocate is guided by core values that must be cultivated and centered in the person's life and work.
- Successful equity leaders and social justice advocates understand the necessity to navigate and negotiate within a system in order to dismantle, correct, and redesign a better system for all of its participants.
- Pruning inaccurate and demoralizing ideologies about self and others is key to the equity leader's ability to reflect and demonstrate dignity, value, and respect even when challenged by the status quo.

Reflection Questions and Ideas to Consider

1. How do the values and competencies of an equity leader and social justice advocate fit into your organizational structure?
2. If you were building the capacity to form allyship, what are the key positions would you need to include to center or advance equity? Who might be best suited for those positions, can also work in collaboration, and can challenge the group to think and act with intentionality and purpose?
3. Considering the importance of sharing a personal belief that speaks to equity. How would you explain and exemplify your personal beliefs, and how have those beliefs helped to form your thinking about self and others?

REFERENCES

Kahneman, D. (2011). *Thinking fast and slow*. New York, NY: Farrar, Straus and Giroux.

Patrick, K., Socal, A., & Ivy, M. (2019). Inequities in advanced coursework: What's driving them and what leaders can do. The Education Trust. https://edtrust.org/wp-content/uploads/2014/09/Inequities-in-Advanced-Coursework-Whats-Driving-Them-and-What-Leaders-Can-Do-January-2019.pdf.

Chapter 4

Humility, Diversity, Equity, and Inclusion (HDEI) Framing

> The absence of humility dishonors the dignity of other people and is a direct reflection of how we see ourselves.
>
> —Candice Dowd Maxwell

There are many commonly known and emerging diversity, equity, and inclusion (DEI) models and frameworks. Each model typically highlights what the research, author, or DEI practitioner deems vital to raise awareness of an issue and correct that issue, especially issues that affect marginalized individuals and communities. Some models follow the traditional DEI components.

In other models, belonging and justice have emerged as trending competencies. While each model has specific underpinnings, all models address the importance of centering and advancing equity—equity being the ultimate goal of DEI work.

This chapter will draw attention to:

- the humility, diversity, equity, and inclusion (HDEI) model for equity leaders and social justice advocates to guide their thinking, action, and behaviors;
- the shifting narratives around social conditions and the effects on education;
- the complexities of humility and why humility is the foundational value;
- the evolution of diversity and trending and emerging thinking about diversity;

- defining inclusion as a product of belonging; and
- developing the conditions for equity and leveraging humility, diversity, and inclusion for equity.

The roadmap to equity, as expressed in this book, starts with humility as the foundation. This proverbial equity roadmap uses humility as leverage to honor diversity, to shape a culture to ensure inclusivity, and to engage in corrective actions that scale toward equity. This framing—humility, diversity, equity, and inclusion (HDEI)—fosters action, yes, but also a shift in the thoughts and behaviors of the individual to articulate a commitment to change and not simply to make a declaration of change.

Figure 4.1 intersects each attribute and the behaviors or actions each attribute cultivates. The following sections will unpack each attribute more deeply and provide critical definitions.

Humility—Dignity
Diversity—Representation
Equity—Leveraging
Inclusion—Belonging

The HDEI model is not necessarily a continuum. It is not organized to encourage someone to move through each attribute in a sequential manner. Instead, I believe that stakeholders, equity leaders, and advocates can use this framing to illustrate how they can activate each element alone or simultaneously to learn new information about other people, themselves, the organization, or an equity issue that needs correcting. It is by cycling through this model that the leader can:

- identify the specific areas of personal growth;
- encourage and motivate themselves and others to be productive; and
- demonstrate values and create the community agreements and practices for the coalition or allyship to form.

That is the essence of the HDEI model.

The framing used for this book and highlighted in this chapter follows the desire to lift equity as the goal. It starts with humility as the critical attribute. Humility, in this instance, serves as a foundation—the

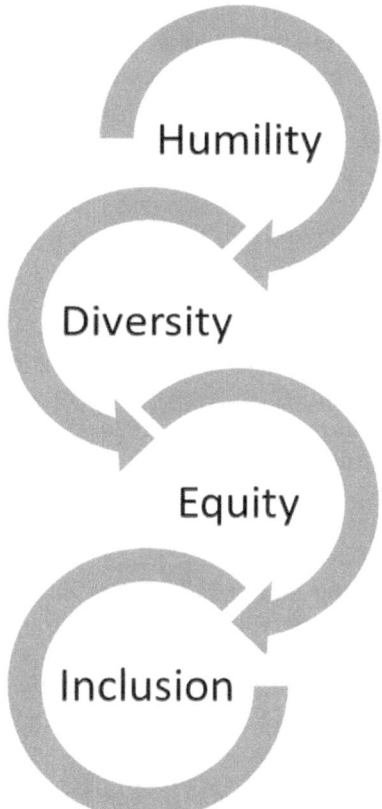

Figure 4.1 HDEI Framework
Source: Author-provided

starting point—because of the interpersonal skills necessary to do the equity work effectively and the reflective nature by which each individual must engage to identify and call out any biases or discriminatory practices and ideologies they hold.

THE COMPLEXITIES OF HUMILITY

Humility is freedom from arrogance, misperceptions about other people, and engaging in harmful conversations and verbal attacks about others (Barnes, Slaton, & Parker, 2020). The nature of humility explores the fragility and vulnerability to acknowledge that an individual, for example, might have limited knowledge or awareness of another's narrative and intersectional story. Humility also emphasizes that regardless of a person's beliefs they respect the dignity of others, value their humanity, articulate a compelling vision as a leader, and engage in inclusive strategies.

In the quote at the beginning of this chapter, I draw on the desire and hope that equity leaders and advocates will honor the dignity of those they are working on behalf of and those with whom they are working in partnership. This act of dignity reflects how a person will interrupt the propensity for arrogance, biases, and stereotypical conditioning that might cause the discriminatory practices to continue.

One of the essential understandings is the need to reckon with how individuals subtly or directly violate the dignity of others through their ideologies, languages, and behaviors. It can be quite disarming when a person engages in an honest reflection of how they might be engaging in harmful or hurtful language and thinking

By constantly tapping into one's sense of humility, they are essentially engaging in a *de-coupling strategy*—a strategy that promotes a shift in thinking to challenge beliefs, values, and ideology that discriminates, negates, and dishonors another person's being. Moreover, from an organizational level, it engages in the remediation and correction of, and the accountability for, any systemic inequity. Thus, the strategy is inextricably aligned to de-biasing. All of this is done with the ultimate goal of shifting a person's thinking, behaviors, and actions toward the greater good of humanity.

Additionally, honoring another person's dignity also means that you have a healthy sense of self. It does not mean you exercise arrogance, but you understand who you are—the gift, graces, and growth opportunities. You also display a sense of confidence, contribute to others in powerful ways, and affirm positivity through language, thinking, and behavior. This means that while someone is constantly pruning their thoughts—de-coupling from negative ways of thinking about others and self—a person is engaging in de-biasing strategies by unpacking their bias boundaries and examining the source of their thinking and behavior.

De-biasing means that a person is engaging cultural humility, civility, and compassion to shift their behavior and actions toward creating a more equitable environment. Micro-affirmations and high-engagement techniques are often used when one is de-biasing. All of this speaks to how different types of oppression work in concert and affect everyone in profound ways.

Four types of oppression—ideological, institutional, interpersonal, and internalized—will be detailed later in this chapter. Before moving further into the discussion, though, it is necessary to highlight why bias boundaries are essential to understand and how those boundaries influence thinking and behaving, specifically what someone believes about other people and how that thinking guides a person's interactions and relationships with others.

Humility requires a person to attend to their *bias boundaries*—the values and beliefs that guide interactions, relationships, and practices (Barnes, Slaton, & Parker, 2020). Bias boundaries can also challenge people to think negatively or positively about their acceptance into specific groups (belonging). These boundaries can also reflect the type of cultural, organizational, and workplace ethos that either affirms or denies belongingness and inclusivity of its members.

In *Humble Leadership: The Power of Relationships, Openness, and Trust*, Schein & Schein (2018) characterize leadership as "a complex mosaic of relationships, not two-dimension (top-down) status in a hierarchy, nor as a set of unusual gifts and talents of 'high-potential' individuals" (p. xi). It is an exciting way to think about leadership development. As an equity leader, exercising humility means cultivating the capacity for relational interdependence to accelerate systemic change and corrective actions. It also means that you are careful and thoughtful in building intergroup trust, candor, and mutual accountability.

Therefore, as an equity leader, you must be willing to maintain an acute focus on both your contributions and the interpersonal dynamics in order to achieve results. Furthermore, being an equity leader means that you position yourself and your team for *social justice advocacy*—a process or state of raising the awareness of, defending a cause of a group, or promoting the interest of a group primarily related to human rights, systemic and structural issues, and the experiences of oppressed, marginalized or underrepresented groups of people.

Humility is complex, yes, and it is an exercise in understanding other people, reflecting on your vulnerabilities, failings, and opportunities for growth. It is an exercise in the intentionality of reckoning with your biases, stereotypes, and internalized messages that trigger the centering of self and the denigration of others.

Certainly, as one thinks about the many ways in which students can access education or not, the social conditioning that makes it difficult for humanity to reckon with its failings, it is easy to see why humility is an essential attribute in making equity leadership and social justice advocacy real and relevant. This commitment and recognition that humility is both a state of being and an action allows you to celebrate, acknowledge, and respect the diversity of those around you and create a valued space that honors their dignity.

DIVERSITY TRENDING

Diversity represents all our varied identities and differences (race, ethnicity, gender, disability, sexual orientation, gender identity, national origin, ability, socioeconomic status, thinking and communication styles, etc.), collectively and as individuals (Just Communities of Arkansas).

I adopted this definition by Just Communities of Arkansas because it includes the commonly recognized categories of diversity and expands the definition to include thinking and communication. This expansion is nuanced because how a person thinks and what they think are directly related to their commitment to change, practice, interact, and design or re-design systems. This definition highlights deeper considerations of diversity, and how research and society has expanded its meaning.

One emerging view about diversity is that focusing on someone's difference does not signal diversity or how they might represent themselves as a part of a larger social and cultural group. Remember that individuals are conditioned to interact, center themselves and others within narrow constructions—social constructions based on the bias boundaries that guide interactions and relationships.

Suppose a school hires four people of color as a part of a diversity cluster hire, a trending practice to recruit and hire diverse talent. That school does so without understanding the fullness of each individual's humanity. It is conceivable that the school has engaged in othering, *otherizing*—an incredibly harmful practice most closely aligned to marginalizing.

Otherizing is often associated with identifying people, especially people of color, as different. The term simply capitalizes on a person's difference to project diversity. This emerging view about diversity does not seek to highlight differences as much as it attempts to highlight the *intersectionality*—how a person's identities overlap to tell an authentic story of who that person is through their experiences, emotionality, and evidence.

It is the narrative that matters most because it is the most honest and accurate accounting of who a person is and who they strive to be. This is why humility is at the forefront of this model and why diversity is a growing and expanding opportunity to understand each person on a deeper level, especially when you avoid the danger of a narrow story about someone else based on your own biases and experiences. In other words, someone's story is theirs to tell you.

In keeping with the example mentioned above, perhaps the school has tokenized these individuals, elevating their race without honoring their dignity or the diversity of their human experiences. *Tokenization* is the act of a person or a group of people selecting someone based on a noticeable or articulated difference, to reflect desired idealized qualities of a majority or dominant culture. Tokenism is sometimes considered covert racism because it gives white people the appearance of being non-racist and of supporting diversity.

Typically, the tokenized person is burdened with the responsibility of representing an entire cultural, racial, oppressed, marginalized, and social group, and recognizes that they are being used as props. Both tokenization and otherizing people can be dangerous, because engaging in these practices forfeits the merit of someone's complete narrative by only focusing on one part of who they are.

Another emerging view or diversity-related trend is the propensity for organizations to engage in diversity window-dressing and creating a diversity boutique. Think about standing outside your favorite store, and the mannequins are dressed in great clothing ensembles. It's eye-catching and presents a good impression of what you expect to find when you enter.

Suppose when you enter the store, they have nothing in your size. The outfit you saw in the window was just a sample, and the workers are rude and do or say nothing that makes you feel welcome and wanted. This is essentially how diversity window-dressing feels and what it looks like when you do not have a sense of belonging. Belonging will be discussed later in this chapter.

As for the diversity boutique, think of it as an abundance of programming and events designed to highlight differences and perhaps diversity, or touts diversity while also claiming that those events and programming address equity. Equity will be detailed in a future section. For now, however, equity is about eliminating obstacles or providing a remedy to a policy or practice that blocks access to opportunities and resources based on diversity or intersectionality of diversity.

Arguably, diversity programming and events do not remedy or redesign a complex system. Instead, it might be used as a way to persuade others to believe equitable change has occurred. It might be a convenient and veiled disguise that allows the system to continue without addressing the real issues of equity within a school.

On the other hand, it could also be a wonderful celebration of representation and solidarity. Schools are particularly good at and have lots of practice celebrating differences through such events and programming. The bottom line is diversity programming, and special events do not always reflect equity.

Therefore, equity leaders and social justice advocates have to be careful in approaching diversity programming and events. While these types of things are great at the face-value level, these programs can quickly fall into the category of window-dressing or just checking off an annual list of things you do to celebrate diversity annually. Remember that a system will operate as it is designed. Therefore, if a practice within the system is to create programming, host special events, and not address inequities, then the system is operating the way it is allowed to operate.

Most schools have decades-long histories of celebrating diversity throughout the school year (i.e., Hispanic Heritage Month, Black History Month, Women's History Month). These diversity acknowledgments have become a normalized part of the standard curriculum in schools while the education system rolls on. With some states' legislative bodies currently passing laws designed to devalue and remove diverse authors, books, and other types of critical literature, these monthly acknowledgments do little to interrupt biased practices in schools.

These events do not necessarily foster a rethinking of a discriminatory policy, nor do these special events influence educators and other stakeholders to think about how the system is faulty and failing marginalized and historically underrepresented students and groups of students.

Mischaracterizing diversity as equity flies in the face of real representational diversity. Real representational diversity is about a person's authentic narrative being respected and valued. Furthermore, referring to diversity window-dressing as equity work is utterly false.

Shifting the thoughts, behaviors, and actions of individuals and organizations to correct discriminatory and biased practices, hold themselves accountable to remove obstacles and barriers, and create new pathways of thinking about access and opportunities to resources, requires more than special events and programs. Equity work requires consistent mental effort that is manifested in personal ideology, institutional policies and practices, and interpersonal development.

A third emerging view is related to the growing diversity within this country and how this ever-increasing demographic influences and demands social change. It has been well reported that the United States is becoming a majority-minority country. And while the racial demography is changing, this change highlights the intersectionality of American's experiences, identities, and humanity. It also speaks volumes about who America is becoming—the citizenry's challenges and the vision for future equity leaders and social justice advocates in education.

It goes without saying that if the country's demography is changing, so will the demographics of schools that are already reportedly majority-minority students. Again, while the demographics have changed within the student body, the faculty body is not representational, nor are those educators as culturally responsive as they might need to be for marginalized and historically underrepresented students.

What is great about the changes in the country's demography is how future generations seem predisposed to work in partnerships with others and build alliances and allyships designed to correct inequities. These groups of mostly young people are well positioned and energized to enact change and demand older generations to acknowledge the need for changes to occur expeditiously. And because those from Generation X to baby boomers are typically the decision-makers and policy-drivers, those particular generations of American educators seem to be the people millennials and Generation Zs are targeting, and frankly, asking the questions, "Why are things still the way they are, and why haven't you done anything more to change it?"

Daringly, these younger generations have demonstrated that they are primed and desire to work together across all diversities, intersectionalities, and differences for one common cause: justice. They have also shown fearlessness and desire to protest, stand in solidarity together, and sound a call for social action and activism.

Many of these young people see beauty in diversity. The few young people following in the footsteps of those who have created bias boundaries around them are pushing against those boundaries to forge new habits of thinking and behaving. It is refreshing to see the emergence of Social Justice 2.0, which I refer to as this generation's Civil Rights Movement, and spotlights the importance of inclusivity.

INCLUSION AS A PRODUCT OF BELONGING

Some models identify belonging as a stand-alone construct. However, for this framing, belonging is in a subordinate position so that an individual and group can achieve real inclusion. I believe that unless you feel welcomed in a space, your participation and comfortability to contribute to a discussion, or even offer ideas for consideration is limited. Belonging creates the conditions for inclusionary actions and behaviors to be articulated and made real to the group members. Therefore, inclusion is a product or perhaps a byproduct of an individual cultivating a culture of belonging.

Belonging is generally defined as a culture where diverse people feel welcome across all of their differences. Both inclusion and belonging are generally manifested and demonstrated through:

- trusting and open relationships;
- critical conversations and dialogues; and
- comfortable and thoughtfully planned physical space.

Inclusion is, then, a culture of belonging where people feel valued and respected. Inclusivity is experienced when people believe that others value their unique and authentic self, their voice, and their way of thinking. At the same time, they feel connected to a group, the intersectionality of their identities, and the narratives they share about those identities are respected.

A precaution about creating a culture of belonging and inclusion is to avoid defaulting to the "seat at the table" ideology without ensuring that the people who are invited to sit at the table are comfortable with the table or even what is being served on the table. Moreover, to make a space truly inclusive with the hopes of making those who enter the space have a sense of belonging, it helps to ask those individuals what a welcoming environment might feel like, look like, and sound like.

Suppose, for example, an organization decides to develop affinity resource groups for its employees without input from the employees about how those groups are formed. In that case, the affinity groups are actually for the employer and not the employees, because their voices—their needs—have not been heard.

In these instances, these types of actions tend to fall under the category of performative and theatrical and are neither substantive nor meaningful. Eventually, the employer-created affinity resource groups fall short of the goal. If an organization asks employees what type of resource group they would like and how they would like them organized, there may be greater buy-in and greater opportunity for success.

The concept works the same in schools and classrooms. The students, staff, parents, and other school professionals should feel like the school is a place where they belong and are included. This might require an evaluation, assessment, or auditing of the quality and effectiveness of curriculum, policies, practices, sports, organization, after school programming, intervention services, disciplinary actions and plans, and so on, to make sure students can access what they need to be successful. Likewise, staff might also need support to shift their thinking, and that shift might come in the form of professional learning opportunities.

For example, restorative justice practices and principles have been used to correct antiquated and biased disciplinary practices and policies that tend to punish students for misbehaving with little opportunities for corrective action and learning, and almost no consideration for cultural difference.

In these instances when students are consistently called out for their behavior, they fail to develop a sense of belonging or inclusion. School becomes a place where they are expected to behave badly—many of these students are referred to special education services for behavior management. Let us revisit Ginsburg Middle School to see how a conversation about a student unfolds between Mr. Walton, a teacher, and Mrs. Wright, the school counselor.

> "Mrs. Wright, Mrs. Wright, I have been meaning to talk with you about Ryan!"
>
> "Hi, Mr. Walton. You caught me just in time before I headed to lunch. What can I do for you?"
>
> "Ryan has been a terror in class for the last couple of weeks, and I could use some insight on some other options. I've sent him to the principal's office several times, and I'm close to sending him to in-school suspension yet again.
>
> "Yes, Mr. Samuels told me that Ryan had been in his office a few times. Have you talked one-on-one with Ryan to see what's going on with him? He's had a lot of family problems over the past year that could be contributing to his behavior in class. I talked with the counselor at his elementary school and he said that Ryan was just a regular kid until his family lost their home."
>
> "Well, I didn't know that and I've tried to talk to him, but his attitude is terrible. He just affects my entire class dynamic. I've dealt with kids like him before, and talking to them doesn't really help. I was actually hoping that you might have some ideas about alternative placements for him."

In this conversation, Mr. Walton has already decided for Ryan what his fate should be, even after learning that he has had a difficult time over the past year. Mr. Walton has allowed his narrowed experiences with other students to color his opinions of Ryan.

This is a classic example of how a student has been disciplined for his behavior several times with little to no positive behavioral support or attempts to prevent further hurt or harm. This type of disciplinary action often becomes the school-to-prison pipeline pathway discussed in chapter 1.

Furthermore, what does this conversation reveal about Ryan's sense of belonging in school and Mrs. Walton's classroom? In these situations, the student is usually very aware of the teacher's feelings toward them. In this case, the fact that Ryan has been sent to the principal's office several times signals that his presence is not desired in the classroom. Depending on the treatment that he might receive from the leadership, Ryan might also believe that he is unwanted in the school.

A point that is sometimes missing in these situations is that even when a student faces disciplinary action or encounters other adverse behaviors from school personnel, the student shows up every day. That could signal that the student is hoping that something will change or that someone will stand up and advocate for them when they cannot.

Therefore, you cannot discount a student who chooses to come to school even under those circumstances. When equity leaders are working toward creating a sense of belonging and inclusion, it is important to acknowledge those critical indicators of trusting relationships, open dialogue, and a physical space that is welcoming and inviting for all students and other stakeholders. And when those elements are positioned within the environment, it makes it easier for leaders and advocates to cultivate a valued and respected conversational space where all parties can be confident and comfortable in exchanging ideas for correction or improvement.

Developing the Condition for Equity to Flourish

In chapter 1, three forms of social conditioning were discussed. Each of these play a role in what people think about themselves and others. The conditions focus how people create and develop institutional policies and practices, how those policies and practices frame their engagements and interactions with each other. The social and cultural conditions also foster positive and negative narratives we manifest in our own lives and within social and cultural groups. These conditionings impact how equity is centered and advanced in our schools and society.

So, what is equity, and how do we develop conditions to achieve equitable outcomes as humble and equity-minded leaders for social justice and change? First, let us focus on the first part of that question: What is equity?

Equity is a structural environment that ensures equality of opportunity and fair treatment in the accessibility of information and resources. It is operationalized when barriers are removed by identifying and eliminating discriminatory policies and practices, and correcting the effects of past discrimination, and ensuring appropriate representation of community members in all spaces.

Equity can be difficult to achieve especially when stakeholders are more interested in maintaining the status quo, instead of leveraging historical privileges, positions, and power for the sake of others. This is where the equity leader's role is critical within an institution once the members of the community have internalized how equity fits into their lives. In order to advance and center equity in a school, the equity leader has to remember and consider implementing five steps.

1. Consistently engage the equity leader values discussed previously and model those values for others.
2. Exercise humility and cultural humility specifically for self-reflection and learn more about the people you are working with.
3. Develop and cultivate the team to diagnose the issue or issues to address.
4. Create a plan or a process to shift mindset and behavior related to the diagnosed issues.
5. Assess and audit the remediation, correction, or remedy for the equity issue.

These five steps provide a big-picture overview to guide the work and the individual's ability to model how equity has been situated and influential in their life. These steps also highlight how equity leaders and social justice advocates create the conditions for equity to flourish.

In part II of this book, I will outline an equity and social change process starting with awareness and moving through a continuum to accountability. Additionally, these steps connect to different types of oppression mentioned earlier in this chapter and the psychology of oppression generally.

Oppression and the Link to Equity

Oppression is an abhorrent failing of humanity. Freire (1970) defines it as a process where one social group in power dehumanizes another social or cultural group and attempts to keep them that way. Furthermore, the oppressed and the oppressor experience the psychological effects of oppression. The oppressed person or group languishes under the weight of being devalued, demoralized, and diminished. Additionally, the oppressor is faced with the fear of losing their sense of superiority—an ideology that is based on the very definition of oppression.

This is one of the primary reasons why individuals who carry historical privileges attempt to protect their values, beliefs, and systems at all cost, even if new information challenges old beliefs or when new information is more logical than the long-held beliefs about a group of people. Many of these same people are often reluctant to engage in social change, equity, and justice. In some ways, it feels like an attempt to hang on to a sense of superiority in a country that is growing increasingly diverse. No human being is superior to another, obviously. However, one person may have more access to resources or may enjoy the benefits of being born into a particular social, cultural group or family.

These psychological effects require the system or the structure to maintain the oppressive ideologies. The system then thrives on the internalized message the oppressed group has accepted about themselves, their place in the world, and their ability to change their circumstances. Remember: the system will do what it is created to do. The educational system is fraught with inequities that start with ideologies carried by all stakeholders and built upon centuries-old history of discrimination, as was discussed in chapter 1.

Types of Oppression

There are four general types of oppression. These types of oppression have emerged over the past several years. Each level reinforces a painful and awful part of human existence. Eliana Pipes, along with Encompass at the Western Justice Center, produced a short video on the four "I's" of oppression. It is titled *Legos and the 4 I's of Oppression* and has been viewed thousands of times. It can be found using the following link: https://youtu.be/3WWyVRo4Uas. It is my go-to video for explaining how these four types of oppression are interrelated.

Systemic and structural inequities and oppression start with our beliefs and values—our ideologies. These ideologies guide our practices and types of policies within our systems. These ideologies attempt to categorize people and communities as inferior or superior. For example, ideologies can label people and groups as destitute or affluent, among many other characterizations.

The institutions or systems created by and based on people's ideologies, power, and influence are then designed to benefit or disadvantage others. These people develop habits and ways of thinking that are normalized into our country's fabric and become the accepted ways of operating. Why? The answer draws upon people's social and cultural conditioning, laws, and policies that can be biased, unjust, and inequitable.

Next is the interpersonal level, which highlights the interactions, behaviors, and anti-relatedness fostered by prejudices, stereotypes, discrimination, microaggressions, and racism. The interpersonal constructs cultivate a sense of superiority or inferiority depending on the social and cultural context in which a person lives. Interpersonal failing can divide communities, segregate people, and perpetuate systemic and structural institutionalized issues and policies.

Lastly is internalized oppression. Internalized messaging is dangerous and hurtful. Essentially, a marginalized group internalizes who they are, what they can accomplish, how they will be treated, and so on, based on the understanding—the narratives imposed upon them by the perceived dominant culture. The blatant oppression experienced by a group for decades and even centuries becomes overt.

In the example above, the teacher projected certain beliefs about a "difficult student" and coded the narrative of rudeness and disorderliness based on his experiences with other students. A *coded narrative* or history accounts for events and attributes that one person projects onto another person based on the individual's experiences, interactions, social and cultural conditioning, and biases.

Coding an individual based on your experience and encounters with others who might look like them, love like them, or live like them robs that individual of telling his/her/their authentic narrative. It also perpetuates bias, prejudice, and discriminatory thinking patterns and can influence people's unwillingness to form trusting relationships with others.

In the sample scenario, Mr. Walton projected a coded narrative onto Ryan. He did not exercise humility to learn more about the student—his background, history, or sense of self. There were no indications that Mr.

Walton attempted to build rapport with Ryan to assess how he might shift the narrative he, Mr. Walton, has created or the internalized messages that Ryan believes about himself. Embedded within this particular school system were practices (i.e., alternative and perhaps unsupportive learning environment or in-school suspension) that might create even more harmful effects than benefits.

Manifestations of Oppression in Schools

These types of oppression are manifested in particular ways in schools and society. Oppression can be blatant, which means that people are consciously engaging in harmful expressions of hatred. It might be a physical attack because of a person's identity. It can be verbal abuse, which is most common. It might be rhetoric about a person or a group of people that causes strife and discord within the student population, and possibly within the staff. However, blatant manifestations of oppression are generally upfront and unveiled threats against the safety and dignity of marginalized and historically discriminated against groups of people. Any form of oppression is hurtful and harmful.

Another way oppression is manifested is by one group benefitting from the oppression of another (Hanna, Talley, & Guindon, 2000). This beneficial type of oppression usually happens through the enforcement of laws, policies, and practices. For example, in chapter 1, I shared incidents where children as young as nine were jailed for seemingly minor behavioral issues. In these cases, the educational and judicial systems were working in cahoots to maintain a system of oppression and created financial gains for the judicial system in those counties.

Betrayal of culture, racial construction, or another identified group because of the marginalization those groups experience is the last way oppression is manifested. In these instances, the individual will denounce or deny who they are, or they will systematically attempt to assimilate or acculturate into the majority or dominant culture to escape the marginalization of their own culture. This betrayal is often predicated on the internalized inferior messages a person receives about who they are, where they come from, what they look like, or their ability. Racially homogenous schools with very few students of color are notorious breeding grounds for denial of one's background, history, and assimilation into the preferred and dominant culture—hoping to "fit in" and be accepted by their peers.

The critical link that binds all of this together is understanding that oppression turns on an axis of power and privilege. *Power* is defined as unequal influence over the distribution of and access to resources, including education, wealth, and citizenship. It is characterized by a collective strength within a group, and power is relational. It is controlled and wielded by one group over another.

Privilege is social, ideological, cultural, and sometimes invisible rights, benefits, and advantages that individuals and groups hold over other individuals and groups. The equity leader and/or the social justice advocate must be ready and willing to leverage their power and privilege to influence change and correction of inequities within the school. When this happens, these leaders are positioning themselves to engage in an equitable and social change process that will be discussed in part II of this book.

In closing, the HDEI framing can be used to help leaders and advocates organize their thoughts and actions around core principles that support equity. The framing can also be used to create some common language and make some informed decisions about what attributes are critically important for schools and organizations. For example, one school might decide to elevate belonging and inclusion in their culture and use diversity as a platform. Another might want to elevate humility and inclusion and use belonging and diversity as subordinate attributes. Whatever the team decides, equity should always be the ultimate goal.

Before moving into the next section, reflect on the questions and ideas presented below, along with the key takeaways for the chapter.

The key takeaways for this chapter are:

- Oppression has historical ramifications on education that have to be corrected and changed in order for students to feel welcomed, included, and deserving of a quality education.
- The HDEI framing can serve as a catalyst for conversation and can help create common language for a team to move forward on their equity journey.
- In order for equity to flourish, leaders have to position themselves and their teams to engage in difficult conversations about the

implications of oppression and the ways in which oppression has been manifested in their schools.

Reflection Questions and Ideas to Consider

1. Based on the types of oppression discussed here, what are some ways in which you have experienced or witnessed the effects of oppression?
2. What specific ways has oppression manifested in your school or organization?
3. How have current events in the country, or your school or community, elevated educational equity?
4. What ideas do you have about using the HDEI framing to influence your team?
5. Consider the pros and cons to using this chapter to have a discussion with your team members. Ask them to think about specific habits of thinking they've had to de-couple and how that de-coupling has enhanced their ability to develop relationships and productive interactions with others.

SELECTED REFERENCES

Barnes, C. D., Rutledge, C., & Parker, T. (2020). *Conflict recovery: Cultural humility and civility in education.* Lanham, MD: Rowman & Littlefield Publishers.

Freire, Paulo (1971) [1970]. *Pedagogy of the oppressed.* Translated by Ramos, Myra Bergman. New York: Herder and Herder. OCLC 1036794065.

Hanna, F., Talley, W., & Guindon, M. (2000). The power of perception: Toward a model of cultural oppression and liberation. *Journal of Counseling and Development,* (78), 430–441.

JCA (2021). Inclusive leadership training. Organizational culture change and leadership development. Retrieved: www.https://www.arkansasjustcommunities.org/amplify/organizational-culture-change-leadership-development/

Schein, E., & Schein, P. (2018). *Humble leadership: The power of relationships, openness, and trust.* Oakland, CA: Berrett-Koehler Publisher, Inc.

PART II

Equitable-Social Change Process Model

Part II will explain and unpack the equitable social change process. Each chapter in this part will:

- draw upon and connect to the first four chapters (part I) of this book;
- provide an equity roadmap of specific strategies, examples, and approaches to measure progress toward meeting equitable strategic outcomes; and
- focus on deepening the equity leader and social justice advocate's knowledge and skills to cultivate an ethos that will support social change in an educational institution.

The equitable social change process was created to provide an equity roadmap to assist in moving a team through four phases toward achieving transformational, equitable, and sustainable change. For example, suppose education institutions expect to be thriving entities where students from all backgrounds feel valued, respected, and advantaged, and where resources, programs, and access to opportunities are open. In that case, these institutions will need to engage in the necessary and challenging work to center and advance equity now. The equitable social change process can serve as a guide to achieving that goal.

The process moves through four phases, as illustrated in Figure 5.1. During each phase, the team explores and examines their role and contribution to the team. They engage in diagnosing inequities and unpacking their authentic narratives for the team and themselves. Next, they

Figure 5.1 Equitable-Social Change Process

work together to develop plans and outcomes to address disparities, and they hold themselves and others accountable for the change. In this last phase, accountability and auditing will monitor the new plans, practices, and policies to determine if any inequities have been replicated and what additional corrections need to be made within the system.

In this part, each chapter is organized much like a workbook. There will be exercises, activities, approaches, and other models to consider that can be used to guide the team's equity efforts. Chapter 5 will focus on awareness and affirmation. Chapter 6 will focus on allyship, advocacy, access, and activism. Chapter 7 will focus on accountability and auditing. Finally, chapter 8 will implicate all educators in a commitment to practice and will end with final thoughts to consider as the reader continues to work for educational equity and justice.

Chapter 5

Awareness and Affirmation

> The paradox of education is precisely this—that as one begins to become conscious, one begins to examine the society in which he is being educated.
>
> —James Baldwin

James Baldwin was one of the greatest novelists and thinkers of his time. He was able to eloquently draw people's attention to the social issues of his day that are unfortunately continuing to plague us today. In this quote, like so much of his work, he strikes a balance of truth and discomfort. As he suggests, this chapter will begin to examine the society in which we live—the educational system—and raise consciousness about issues and concerns while also affirming collective diversity.

Chapter 5 will:

- discuss historical and contemporary issues in P–12 education and in teacher education programs;
- discuss the long-term effects of inequities on individuals and groups of people;
- present ideas, activities, and strategies to raise awareness, affirm each other's humanity through collective narrative and storytelling, and shift the conversation toward equitable practices; and
- provide an overview of phase 1 of the equitable social change process.

While many issues could be discussed, the issues highlighted in this chapter focus on the intersection of race, educational equity, socioeconomics, gender, and, to some degree, the impact of the COVID-19 pandemic on education. These more global educational equity issues are affecting education at every level. While there may be more specific inequities you will want to address in your respective school and organization, this discussion will provide some context for deeply rooted and large-scale issues affecting schools at the local level.

Throughout this chapter, there are reflective questions to examine what social justice issues are essential to you, how the global issues presented in this chapter might affect your respective school and community, and how equity is critical to solving many of society's challenges. There will also be ideas and suggested activities that equity leaders can utilize to facilitate or engage in conversations about the issues presented later in this chapter, or the issues that equity leaders and team members diagnose within their schools and organizations.

Let us begin with an overview of phase!—awareness and affirmation—and then discuss key issues related to the intersection of race, education, and socioeconomic status of various stakeholders in education. Each of the issues discussed later is persistent and affects a large swatch of the educational diaspora. It is important to raise awareness about these issues at the federal, state, and local school level if the changes and corrections are sustainable and rooted in the fabric of the education system globally.

EQUITABLE-SOCIAL CHANGE PROCESS (ESCP) PHASE 1: AWARENESS AND AFFIRMATION

In chapter 3, I presented the core values of an equity leader. Those values, humility, responsive decision-making, compassion, and capacity-building are all necessary to ensure phase 1 is sufficiently implemented. However, it is important to understand that standing in solidarity with someone is only a small part of the equity leader's role. This person, or these persons, must also be prepared for the deep work of social change, which sometimes is very slow and arduous, but satisfying.

This first phase of the ESCP sets the stage for the equity efforts to advance. In this phase, there are four actions the equity leader needs to engage to increase their awareness and affirm the narratives of others:

1. Exercise cultural humility, which will allow you to honor the narratives of others and engage in ongoing self-reflection. This is probably the most significant part of phase 1 because it enables you to think about yourself as an influencer, learner, and equity facilitator. Because it is also highly relational, you are also modeling sensitivity, vulnerability, and honoring the authentic narratives of others.

Coded narratives must be discarded during this phase. Using an exercise like What's on the Table, which was introduced in the book *Conflict Recovery: Cultural Humility and Civility in Education* (2020), which I coauthored, participants can intersect specific identities and share stories affirming or challenging those identities. For example, what is the story or your narrative as a Latina–educator–crime novelist? The idea is, what someone thinks of you has little to do with you and speaks more about their own beliefs about you or who you are as a member of a cultural and/or social group and their cultivated experiences with other people who might share this identity.

2. Source and examine your biases, beliefs, and values to determine how you might effectively model equity through your thinking and behavior. This is a preventative step that might help you avoid replicating inequitable behavior. It allows you to prune your biases and maintain a sense of compassion and humility.

To source your biases means that you unpack where these values come from, how you came to hold certain beliefs, and engage reflective thinking to determine and reckon with thoughts, emotions, and tensions engaging in this type of de-coupling might cause. This is a daily practice.

3. Review data from various sources to diagnose the inequities that need correction. This data review will allow you to narrow your work to focus on a specific issue. For most people, many issues will emerge that require correction. However, trying to focus on too many issues can become overwhelming and lead to stagnation or halt progress altogether.

4. Increase and enhance your consciousness about the issue. This might mean you will need to engage in professional learning, research, or cultivating valued conversations with others about the issues in your respective school or organization.

In this step, you also want to determine what contributions individuals can make to the process and the strengths, rewards, and weaknesses of, and challenges and threats to, focusing on this issue—using either a SWOT analysis or SCARF analysis. The SCARF analysis, developed by David Rock (2008), focuses on five levels to assess threats and rewards at each level.

DIFFICULT CONVERSATIONS ABOUT RACE (IN SCHOOL)

Race is probably one of the most polarizing and uncomfortable topics to discuss in any setting. A major contributing factor to the uncomfortableness is that race has not been normalized as a topic of discussion. Typically, when the subject of race comes up, people will default to prepared responses, attempt to shut down conversations, or engage in protectionism and ignorance.

One of the most controversial topics in education is whether or not to teach race-consciousness content. The issue is so volatile that school boards, school leaders, state legislators, and even federal government officials have weighed in on the topic. Yet, no subject has created more dissension—more debate—within the current educational mainstream than Critical Race Theory (CRT).

The most interesting part of the debate is that Critical Race Theory is not taught in P–12 schools. Critical Race Theory is a theory that promotes an examination of how race impacts the policies, practices, and processes within a system or structure. The contemporary theory was introduced by Kimberlé Crenshaw, Richard Delgado, and Derrick Bell decades ago and has most often been taught in graduate school and, more specifically, law schools to examine the role race plays in the judicial system. Over the years, the theory has evolved to include more identity intersections.

Still, the theory is not taught in public school. Imagine a first-grade teacher trying to discuss with six- and seven-year-olds how race has impacted laws and policies, and creates systemic inequities. Typically, the scope of race-conscious teaching happens during race-based history months. For decades, Black History Month was relegated to educators teaching a lesson or two about Martin Luther King Jr., Ruby Bridges, Harriet Tubman, or a contemporary figure like Oprah Winfrey or President Barack Obama.

In "A Lesson on Critical Race Theory," written by Janel George (2021) for the American Bar Association's *Human Rights Magazine*, she states,

> CRT is not a diversity and inclusion "training" but a practice of interrogating the role of race and racism in society that emerged in the legal academy and spread to other fields of scholarship. Crenshaw—who coined the term "CRT"—notes that CRT is not a noun, but a verb. It cannot be confined to a static and narrow definition but is considered to be an evolving and malleable practice. It analyzes how the social construction of race and institutionalized racism perpetuate a racial caste system that relegates people of color to the bottom tiers. CRT also recognizes that race intersects with other identities, including sexuality, gender identity, and others. CRT recognizes that racism is not a bygone relic of the past. Instead, it acknowledges that the legacy of slavery, segregation, and the imposition of second-class citizenship on Black Americans and other people of color continue to permeate the social fabric of this nation. (n.p.)

Most people in the debate demanding that CRT be eliminated from the school's curriculum have limited knowledge of the theory. They also have limited understanding of how researchers use the approach to examine and explore how race subjugates a person's dignity and how the systems and structures in this country are inherently biased and discriminatory. This level of critical analysis of racial bias, hate, and discrimination is simply not taught in P–12 schools.

Perhaps though, Critical Race Theory should be taught in, at least, high schools. This would help normalize the conversation about race so that people can begin to shift their thinking to correct inequities within the system that allow race to determine a person's worth, values, intelligence, importance, and access to resources and opportunities.

An elementary school principal shared the following conversation with me. This brief conversation examples the disinformation around

Critical Race Theory and the concern about something that does not exist in P–12 school curricula.

> *Parent: Are you planning to teach Critical Race Theory in school? I am totally against it, and I don't want my child exposed to that nonsense.*
>
> *Principal: Well, tell me exactly what you think Critical Race Theory teaches, and I'll confirm if we are teaching that in school.*
>
> *Parent: (Silence.)*

Most individuals do not learn about Critical Race Theory until college, graduate school, or, more often than not, during their doctoral studies in specific fields. This debate is another issue snared by misinformation or disinformation in a long line of problems. It has been stoked, weaponized, and politicized into a dreadful monster meant to drive fear and hate. The fear is understandable because of the mountains of confusing information. It is argued that some people fear what the younger generation will do with the truth about the history in America.

Proponents of Critical Race Theory believe that it is about examining the truths and reality of the systems and structures in America that discriminate, criminalize, and devalue people of color, specifically, and other individuals from marginalized groups. Critical Race Theory can help to unpack and draw awareness to a complete history of American Descendants of Slaves (ADOS), slave owners, immigrants and naturalized citizens, and undocumented individuals as human beings working to thrive within systems that will treat them with kindness and respect, or not.

The understandable fear of telling a full history of America and the systems and structures that have created haves and have nots—systems that advantage some people while disadvantaging others—is not the history many want to be told. Some people prefer the narrative that I call the "Gone with the Wind Glory"—an ode to the movie. It is a romanticized history, like the antebellum South. It is a history that boasts riches and land ownership while at the same time making the lives of enslaved people seem somehow bearable, or even comical.

There is so much tragedy and disassociation with that painful part of the American experiment, which is slavery. It is understandable why some people in positions of power would prefer not to address the guilt and shame of slavery and the continued trauma of American slavery.

Still, history deserves a complete and thorough review. How constitutional ideologies and institutions in America have robbed many people of their opportunity to be exceptional, simply based on their skin color, is shameful. Yet, many of those same people have managed to work through those obstacles—and have navigated and negotiated systems to reach a desired level of achievement.

However, the pathways to those achievements were littered with broken barriers and discarded obstacles that should have never been allowed to block the path. This is why shattering the system is necessary. Equity leaders must stand up and urgently call others into a conversation about how they will work together to shift and change the system. They must ensure that obstacles and barriers are eliminated, even if that means they will have to scrub—de-couple—their biased ideologies and discriminatory practices.

For example, in 2021, the National Association of School Psychologists released a position statement titled *The Importance of Addressing Equity, Diversity, and Inclusion in Schools: Dispelling Myths About Critical Race Theory*. In this document, the association provides an overview of Critical Race Theory. In addition, the association corrects misinformation about the theory and other controversial subjects like culturally responsive teaching. This association, like others, is taking a stand to lead and provide learning opportunities and information to counter the negative and divisive messaging about these topics. This association also linked their position against banning such teaching to their organizational standards of ethics.

Taking the path of least resistance to understanding history fails to recognize both humanity's indignities and its brilliance. Critical Race Theory simply promotes a thorough examination of how race has influenced laws, policies, and practices. It is a framework that helps facilitate discussion and acknowledge how colleagues, neighbors, parents, students, and friends have been denied opportunities because of their racial construction. The theory should not be used as a battering ram against educators who desire to teach a complete history, nor should it be used to plant fear and division in the futures of young people.

Other Race-Related Issues in Education

Critical Race Theory is trending, and so it is important to highlight the misinformation surrounding the theory, culturally responsive teaching, and a host of other race-conscious teachings. This would include legislation to ban books, literary giants like Toni Morrison, and journalistic projects like the 1619 project. In addition, some states have moved to ban diversity and inclusion professional development for educators. Others propose limiting content about Dr. Martin Luther King Jr. and other civil rights activists. And if this is not enough, some other long-standing race-related constructs have starved transformational educational equity from taking root.

One such construct is color-blindness. Color-blindness is the idea that race does not affect a person's standing in society or how that person might be treated or viewed. Color-blind racial ideology (CBRI) is a widely held belief that skin color plays a role in interpersonal interactions and institutional policies and practices. Carr introduced CBRI in 1997. Since then, the theory has been used to explain the harmful nature of phrases like, "I don't see color," or "I treat everyone the same regardless of their color." These are two common refrains used to avoid uncomfortable conversations about race. Furthermore, these phrases are not factual and negate a part of an individual's identity and the narratives they might tell about how their racial construction is an important part of their narrative—their background, history, and intersectionality.

Ironically, the idea of color-blindness is connected to the idealized and historical speech given by Dr. Martin Luther King Jr. Over the years, the idea of color-blindness has been attached to a specific line in his speech where he idealizes a different country for his children to live—a country where skin color is not a factor in their futures. Unfortunately, this part of his speech has been deconstructed and decontextualized to mean something entirely different than the context of his original remarks.

Living in a world where we are not judged by our skin color but on character is aspirational, and it is also an inaccurate account of the current world and the country we live in. That is the actual context of what Dr. King said in his speech. Meaning, it would be wonderful if the ideal world he spoke about was a reality. Sadly, it is not, and unfortunately, humanity continues to strive to create such a world.

Neville, Awad, Brooks, Flores, and Bluemel (2013) identify several forms of color-blindness. One form is called *color-evasion*, which was introduced through Frankenberg's (1993) work involving denying racial differences, emphasizing sameness, the reluctance of white and people of color to benefit from diverse relationships and increased microaggressions.

Color-evasion seems to have two purposes. First, it is an aspirational and philosophical goal intended to reduce prejudice, discrimination, and unfair treatment of people of color. Second, it represents the belief in sameness or a philosophy that we are all human beings under the skin.

I suggest that it is impossible not to notice a person's race and touting perspectives and the false belief that color-blindness is relevant and attainable does not support justice and equity, nor does color-blindness eliminate bias or discrimination. On the contrary, it might create conditions for more biased behaviors and increased discomfort with conversations about race.

As the reader thinks about increasing awareness or becoming more aware of the conditions creating educational inequities, it is essential to have some baseline data and information about the impact of race in schools. Conversations about race in school can help normalize and address how race has been codified in policies, practices, laws, and so forth, affecting all students, especially students of color, LGBTQIA+ individuals, and girls.

Normalizing Race Talk and Codification of Race

Talking about race is not a normalized practice. It is uncomfortable and challenging to discuss. Talking about race heightens emotions, tensions, and fears. Yet, race has been codified in institutions, policies, interpersonal relationships, and friendships, how schools are funded, and so on. The codification has led to internalizing racism and race-based ideologies of white people and people of color of all ethnicities, backgrounds, genders, and gender identities.

Race is a social and cultural construction that people have adopted as a part of their identity. Blackness and whiteness have become the expression of cultural identities and positions of power, excellence, affinity, and acceptance. The acceptance of Blackness and white identity can be informative and reflective.

However, no biological structural connection to these cultural phenomena determines if one group is better than another. Those are social and cultural ideologies baked into the fabric of the society and are founded on principles of superiority and inferiority—who is worthy of dignity and who is not.

There is just so much to unpack about race and the centuries-old narratives and ideals about access to power, historical privileges—both race and gender. The last point for this section is a brief discussion of how race intersects with a person's lived experience and how race is often conflated with socioeconomic status. These concepts are prevalent in schools and often dictate how students are treated fairly and unfairly.

People, in general, are racially biased. The fact is that depending on where you live, the people in your community—in your family, the folks you develop friendships with, go to church with, play sports with, go to schools with, and so on—are pretty homogenous. So most people have to be intentional about diversifying their circles of influence.

In a recent conversation with a group of young women who were members of a predominantly white sorority, one of these young women asked, "what can I do to make things better for other people?" The answer was simple yet complex and potentially created a moment of reflection and cognitive dissonance for this young woman. The answer was, "Evaluate your circle of friends and acquaintances. If everyone looks like you, comes from a similar background, and thinks like you, you essentially have a narrowed view of the world. Also, be intentional about how you leverage your privilege and show up in solidarity—authentically and consistently to events and programs that highlight diversity. Leverage the power of this sorority to call attention to a policy or practices that need to change and do so in partnership with marginalized and historically underrepresented peers on your campus."

It was a lot to take in for this young woman. However, as someone open to learning how best to advocate for change and engage in equitable strategic outcomes, this young woman hopefully reckoned that the extraordinary power of working in solidarity with other people could effect change and promote inclusion.

In that same meeting, another young woman was trying to understand why her friend, who was a person of color, became so upset with her following the events during the summer of 2020 immediately following the killing of many unarmed Black men, particularly George Floyd.

The answer was, "Avoid centering yourself in your friend's trauma and understand that she is upset and angry about the circumstances—the events—the tragedies that were arguably racially motivated. Moreover, understanding and empathizing with the fact that she might also be frustrated by what your whiteness and white identity represent and what her Black identity and Blackness represent outside of your friendship."

These conversations are never easy, but they become easier when equity leaders and advocates normalized and centered race as cause for inequities. For most marginalized people, when others recognize and acknowledge the crushing history of racialized atrocities and how those atrocities continue to haunt humanity, that acknowledgment might foster a willingness to share experiences—stories that have either affirmed or challenged their identities.

Another broad issue that intersects race and gender is the challenge of creating a more diverse educator workforce. This issue delves into the historical bias that influences educators' behaviors, the type of instruction and curriculum provided to students, where teachers are educated, and where teachers from different racial backgrounds find employment. Before moving to the next issue, reflect on the following questions.

Reflection Questions

1. If you were asked to tell a story about how your race has influenced your access to opportunities, what stories would you share?
2. What are the policies around race-conscious teaching in your school, and how do those policies support diversity or the white-washing of the curriculum?
3. How would you begin to normalize conversations about race, and what additional information or support would help you normalize those conversations?
4. Based on the four steps of phase 1, which will be the most challenging for you, and why? What can you do to lessen the tension around that step?

THE MAJORITY WHITE EDUCATOR LABOR FORCE CHALLENGE

In an address at Howard University, Education Secretary Edward King Jr., as cited in the *State of Racial Diversity in the Educator Workforce* report (2016), shared with the audience that

> Diversity is inherently valuable. We are stronger as a nation when people of varied backgrounds, experiences, and perspectives work and learn together; diversity and inclusion breed innovation. Groups of more diverse problem solvers have been found to outperform groups of less diverse problem solvers, and companies with more diversity in their leadership also tend to be top financial performers. Research shows that diversity in schools, including racial diversity among teachers, can provide significant benefits to students. While students of color are expected to make up 56 percent of the student population by 2024, the elementary and secondary educator workforce is still overwhelmingly white. In fact, the most recent US Department of Education Schools and Staffing Survey (SASS), a nationally representative survey of teachers and principals, showed that 82 percent of public-school teachers identified as white. This figure has hardly changed in more than fifteen years; data from a similar survey conducted by the department in 2000 found that 84 percent of teachers identified as white. Improving teacher diversity can help all students. Teachers of color are positive role models for all students in breaking down negative stereotypes and preparing students to live and work in a multiracial society. A more diverse teacher workforce can also supplement training in the culturally sensitive teaching practices most effective with today's student populations. (*State of Racial Diversity in the Educator Workforce* p. 1)

The *State of Racial Diversity in the Educator Workforce* report (2016) revealed that the percentage of white students was decreasing and the students of color was increasing, and by 2024 the majority of students in public schools would be of color. Specifically, by 2024 54 percent of students would identify as a person of color, and Latinx students in public school are increasing in number faster than other groups within the BIPOC diaspora. Yet, the educator workforce remains predominantly white, as it has for the past two or more decades.

In elementary and secondary schools, the educators, teachers, and leaders are overwhelmingly white. Teachers and leaders of color have increased slightly; however, white teachers outpace educators of color by significant margins. While being a teacher who happens to be white on the surface is not an issue. The lack of cultural responsiveness and preparedness to teach a growing diverse student body is the issue and the historical racial biases that all are bringing into the school environment.

Additionally, white students enroll in teacher education and preparation programs and graduate at a higher rate than students of color. The authors assert that while 73 percent of white students complete their bachelors in education, only 42 percent of Black and 49 percent of Latino students complete their undergraduate degree in education.

However, the statistics are different when looking at historically Black colleges and universities (HBCUs) and alternative certification programs. In contrast, HBCUs generally enroll 2 percent of prospective teacher candidates of color. On the other hand, those institutions enroll 16 percent of Black teacher candidates. Those seeking alternative routes are overwhelmingly people of color.

What is also compelling is where teachers of color find employment. The majority of this group of teachers will find employment in predominantly minority schools in low wealth communities. According to the report, these schools hired 63 percent white, 17 percent Black, and 16 percent Latinx teachers as opposed to schools in higher-income and affluent communities. In those communities, there is a stark difference. Teachers of schools in higher-income communities are 93 percent white and 6 percent are Black and Latinx. As for leaders and principals, more than 80 percent are white.

It is important to recognize that the teacher and educator pipeline begins to collapse almost from the start. Potential candidates faced multiple roadblocks that, for some, are insurmountable. The roadblocks could be anything from a singular pathway to admission to biased admissions tests and policies to high standards and low support. It could also be interpersonal ideologies about who belongs and who does not belong in the profession.

Therefore, many students of color who cannot navigate those systems forfeit their dream or seek alternative routes to teaching beyond traditional teacher education programs. So the questions that you might be asking are: Why is the racial construction of teachers important in the classroom and this discussion; and, Does this mean that white people should not be teaching students of color?

The answer to the last part of that question is no. Diversity in all forms is critical to helping students feel welcomed, supported, and that they belong. Each student and educator can learn so much more about themselves and others when the environment is more diverse. Additionally, given the institutional structures that has lifted whiteness, not white people as a group, but whiteness as a racialized superiority construct, it can be quite affirming for students of color, and other marginalized students, to see representations of themselves in the classroom and school.

We must also consider how teachers from all backgrounds—including racial and social constructions—are prepared for an increasingly diverse and complex classroom. So, representation is important to answer the first part of the question. Also, ensuring the educators are well prepared to meet the challenges of diverse demography is equally critical.

However, as a side note, I am also critical of teachers of color who have adopted biased and discriminatory ideologies about students of color. Some of these teachers may be traumatized by internalized racism, so much so that they, too, are marginalizing students. This next issue will intersect race, gender, socioeconomics, and equity. Reflect on the questions below before moving to the next section.

Reflection Questions

1. What is the racial composition of your staff, and how would your students and staff benefit from an increased or broader racial and cultural diversity composition of staff?
2. What tensions do you need to resolve about creating a more diverse educator workforce? How can you de-center yourself in that thinking, so that you avoid defaulting to the status quo?
3. What factors have created the conditions for your school's staff composition to be homogeneous or diverse? Are there specific ideologies and beliefs that guide policies, practices around hiring that have created barriers for diversity?

EARLY CARE AND EARLY CHILDHOOD EDUCATION DISPARITIES

The early childhood years are arguably the most critical and formidable years during an individual's lifespan. From birth to five years, developmental areas are fortified with various learning opportunities as children transition into elementary school. Unfortunately, while these children are often taught by some of the most dedicated, compassionate, and committed teachers, they are also taught by some of the lowest paid, under-, and unprotected members of the educators' workforce.

The early care and education workforce is predominantly Women of Color who continue to be the lowest wage earners in education across the country. They typically make far less than their public school counterparts and receive fewer benefits, including sick leave and health insurance. While federal and state-funded programs fare better than privately operated schools and centers, the wage gap is still significant. Moreover, structural inequities are baked into the system.

In 1938, the Fair Labor Standards Act did not include Black and brown women who were domestic help and often cared for white children from middle-income and affluent families (Schilder & Curenton, 2021). These women were excluded from receiving minimum wages and other benefits. In addition to other systemic issues that intersect with race (i.e., housing, health care, education, etc.), these women continue to be underpaid and often undervalued. These Black and brown early childhood educators, unlike their white counterparts, are less likely to work in school-based early childhood programs that offer better compensation and benefits.

While the issue of salary and benefits is one these women face, another issue is the lack of education and credentialing opportunities, which are recognized by state departments of education and can position these women for higher-paying positions. Unfortunately, these credential and teacher education programs are often out of reach for many women. They may need child care, flexible hours, and financial support to enroll in such programs.

The fact that these women are too often low-wage earners means it is a vicious cycle that precludes them from pursuing such opportunities and increasing their ability to care for their families. Therefore, state and national efforts are needed to address these and other related issues.

Four primary shifts can address inequities in the early childhood workforce:

1. Eliminate policies that underserve this population within the workforce.
2. Redesign policies that advance equity for the teachers and the children they teach. Many states—including Alabama, Iowa, Missouri, California, and Michigan—are working to correct inequities by offering loan forgiveness, prioritizing racial equity in early childhood, convening councils, and task forces to address funding and access.
3. Engage in research to support the need to eliminate racial inequities in early childhood education.
4. Evaluate new policies to make sure those policies have not caused more inequity.

These types of state-level efforts and the federal response to these issues will highlight the need to uproot the inequities and plant seeds of equity. Additionally, the learning loss experienced by many students from the COVID-19 pandemic adds another layer of inequities that must be addressed.

Therefore, creating or correcting policies and laws that will allow early childhood educators to be treated fairly, have access to educational programming that will position and prepare them to teach and support the children and families, and earn a living wage is overdue.

In addition to the issues discussed in detail, many other issues deserve attention and awareness and are profoundly affecting students, especially those in public education. Those issues include:

- preparing educators to be culturally responsive for diverse student demography;
- overrepresentation of students of color in special education for behavioral issues;
- adultification of girls and young women of color in P–12 and higher education;
- lack of resources for ESOL and ELL students;
- support for undocumented students and families;

- support for students who identify as LGBTQIA+, including effective counseling and professional learning for educators and others;
- increasing the diversity of students in advanced placement and gifted and talented programs;
- addressing biases and discriminatory admissions and testing policies and practices in teacher education;
- acknowledging the conflation of race and socioeconomic status perpetuates historical racial narratives;
- eliminating practice and policies that demoralize Black and Latino boys in school;
- addressing unfair and biased disciplinary practices and behavioral interventions that primarily affect students of color;
- recalling bans on race- and gender-conscious teaching in schools, and calling for more race- and gender-conscious education;
- addressing the lack of diverse faculty in teacher education programs;
- centering equity before or while promoting special events and diversity programming;
- increasing support and teaching of culturally responsive mental health approaches for counselors;
- evaluating testing bias affecting P–12 students and teacher candidates;
- implementing restorative justice principles and practices to support peace and justice;
- creating learning circles and affinity groups for students, staff, and others about race and other challenging topics;
- revising school curricula to promote diversity and inclusion; and
- promoting opportunities and access for both trade school and college equally, fairly, and without bias.

In addition to raising awareness around the various issues, it is also important to unpack why equity is important to you, what your experiences are with inequities, and engage in sharing that equity story with others who might become a part of your allyship.

Knowing and Affirming Your Equity "Why"

Simon Sinek started a movement to inspire individuals to find their "why" with his books *Start with Why: How Great Leaders Inspire*

Everyone to Take Action (2011), and later in *Find Your Why: A Practical Guide for Discovering Purpose for You and Your Team* (2017). These books have been used widely across many disciplines and career paths. As it relates to equity, this discovery of the why can be critical to how one amplifies their personal commitment to equity and the work they do to achieve equity. Knowing why equity is central in your life allows you to articulate a clear vision and mission. It can also help unpack the experiences that drive your commitment to equity.

Discovering your equity "why"—your equity story—can be a reflective exercise that activates memories, explores your feelings, and projects your core value. For example, imagine engaging in such an activity—an activity that simply asks the question, "why?" This exercise was first introduced to me through the Disruptive Equity Education Project (DEEP), founded by Dr. Darnisa Amante-Jackson. You can learn more about DEEP at https://digdeepforequity.org.

Reflect on the dialogue below between Kim and Terrance to examine how Kim filtered her response through each "why" level Terrance asked.

Facilitator: This next exercise is designed for you to unpack why equity is important to you, and to your work and organization. Kim, you will start by thinking of your response to that question. Terrance, your role in this exercise is to simply ask why. You will ask Kim why five times. At the end, Terrance you will recall and share what you heard Kim recount was her journey through the whys to make sure you have the correct iteration. Let's get started.

Terrance: Kim, why is equity important to you?

Kim: It's important to ensure that people have access to resources and can live life to their fullest potential.

Terrance: Why?

Kim: Because it's not fair to treat people differently or lock them out of opportunities because of who they are and what they look like.

Terrance: Why?

Kim: This has been an ongoing fight. It's not who we should be, and it infuriates me.

Terrance: Why?

> Kim: I have experienced discrimination and I know how hurtful being treated as less than can be. I wouldn't want anyone to experience that and where I can use my life experience to create change, I will.
>
> Terrance: So, what I heard you say is you have experienced discrimination and those experiences affected you in a way that you wouldn't want anyone else to endure. Also, you acknowledge that access is not afforded to all and that is something you think should change and you want to be a part of that change process.

In this example, Kim filters through her feelings and thinking about equity and her experiences with discrimination. Typically, this activity becomes increasingly difficult as you work your way through to the core why. The last why is where most individuals will reveal their vulnerability and speak about equity from a very personal perspective.

The other crucial part of this activity is the role of the partner to be present in the moment and listen for understanding. Overall, this can be an incredibly powerful exercise. It can also be a catalyst for developing your equity bio and personalizing your equity title.

An equity bio is a description of how you engage in equity work. It describes your pathway toward advancing equity, and it speaks directly to how you will embrace your influence for change. It is not an *ally resume*. An ally resume is a list of events, initiative, programs, and so on, that an ally of a marginalized group has participated in. Usually, the ally resume is introduced into a conversation when a perceived threat that questions someone's *wokeness* is at hand.

Wokeness is a colloquial term that began in communities of color as early as the 1920s. The term was firming rooted in the cultural consciousness of present-day generations of people of color after the murder of Michael Brown in 2014. The term gained sociopolitical capital was co-opted outside of communities of color and infused into the mainstream consciousness. The original meaning was a call for people of color, particularly Black people, to become socially conscious and aware.

It became a rallying cry for the Black Lives Matter movement and other race- and gender-conscious movements and was reintroduced through social media, music, and movies. Throughout the years, the term has generally maintained its original content. However, like many Black vernacular phrases, "stay woke" has become a polarizing phrase. It is also used as a counter-message to cancel culture. In 2020, *Vox*

Table 5.1 Examples of Equity Titles and Bios

Source: Author-created

Title	Bio
social change strategist	Influence policies and practices for others.
justice education teacher	Teaching young people about their rights.
equity advocate	Creating opportunities for fairness and impartiality.
inclusion and equity leader	Managing and disrupting systems for change.
good troublemaker	Bringing awareness to voting rights issues.

published an interesting report by Aja Romano on the history of woke, wokeness as a "watchword" for spotlighting deception and social and racial animus.

I have used all of these activities and exercises in my consultancy work. These activities or exercises are an opportunity for individuals to think about their commitment to equity and equity work, how equity is internalized in their lives, and develop a bio—a description of their work toward advancing and centering equity and justice for others. These activities encourage individuals to think deeply about how they would characterize and operationalize the principles of equity.

The equity title takes it one step further to provide an accurate depiction of who they are in the fight for equity and what they can contribute as a DEI representative. I asked a number of individuals who self-report working in the diversity, equity, and inclusion space to describe, in six words or less, their equity bio and what title they might give themselves. Table 5.1 highlights some of their responses.

In closing, there are hosts of issues that equity leaders and advocates may urgently want to focus on in their respective organizations. The issues presented in this chapter may resonate and provide a contextual frame for the larger, and in some instances, contemporary, issues that the educational system is facing. Equity leaders and advocates must create and cultivate a *valued conversational space* where individuals feel confident in contributing their ideas and perspectives, and engaging in a dialogue and conversation.

The conversational space is not declarative but a commitment to cultivating respect and honoring the dignity of others. This becomes the space where groups of people can come together for greater understanding, empathize with other people's authentic narratives, and begin to cultivate belonging so that everyone's voice is heard and welcomed in the space. Reflect on the questions below and the key chapter takeaways to make connections with your equity leadership efforts.

The key chapter takeaways are:

- Leaders must raise their and others' consciousness around the inequities in their schools and organizations using all available data to determine the next steps. This increase in awareness also fosters how the group will move into the subsequent two phases of the equitable social change process, allyship and advocacy, and access and activism.
- Equity leaders and social justice advocates leading equity efforts must be ready to demonstrate vulnerability and engage in difficult conversations about issues of inequity within the community and work to diagnose issues of inequity in their school.

Reflection Questions

1. Why should all educators be concerned about early childhood educators' disparities?
2. What additional shifts would you add to the list that might correct the inequities and disparities early childhood educators face?
3. What additional issues would you add to the present list in your school, community, or state? What work has already been done on those issues that you and your team can build on?
4. Why is the first phase—awareness and affirmation—critical to centering, advancing, and transforming schools for equity?

SELECTED REFERENCES

Barnes, C. D., Rutledge, C., & Parker, T. (2020). *Conflict recovery: Cultural humility and civility in education.* Lanham, MD: Rowman & Littlefield Publishers.

Department of Education (2016, July). The state of racial diverse educator workforce. https://www2.ed.gov/rschstat/eval/highered/racial-diversity/state-racial-diversity-workforce.pdf.

Frankenberg, R. (1993). *White women, race matters: The social construction of whiteness.* Minneapolis, MN: University of Minnesota Press.

George, J. (2021, January 11). A lesson on Critical Race Theory. *Human Rights Magazine*. National Bar Association. https://www.americanbar.org/groups/crsj/publications/human_rights_magazine_home/civil-rights-reimagining-policing/a-lesson-on-critical-race-theory/.

National Association of School Psychologists. (2021). *The Importance of addressing equity, diversity, and inclusion in schools: Dispelling myths about Critical Race Theory* [handout].

Neville, H. A., Awad, G. H., Brooks, J. E., Flores, M. P., & Bluemel, J. (2013). Color-blind racial ideology: Theory, training, and measurement implications in psychology. *American Psychologist, 68*(6), 455–466. https://doi.org/10.1037/a0033282.

Schilder, D., & Curenton, S. (2021, January 29). Policymakers can redesign the early childhood and education system to root out structural racism. *Urban Wire* (blog, Urban Institute). https://www.urban.org/urban-wire/policymakers-can-redesign-early-childhood-and-education-system-root-out-structural-racism.

Sinek, S. (2011). *Start with why: How great leaders inspire everyone to take action*. London: Penguin Publishing.

Sinek, S. (2017). *Find your why: Discovering purpose for you and your team*. London: Penguin Publishing.

Rock, D. (2008). A brain-based model for collaborating and influencing others. *Neuroleadership Journal,* (1), 1–10. https://coe.uga.edu/assets/downloads/dei/internal-resources/conflict-scarf.pdf.

Romano, A. (2020, October 9). A history of "wokeness." Stay woke: How a Black activist watchword got co-opted in the culture war. *Vox*. https://www.vox.com/culture/21437879/stay-woke-wokeness-history-origin-evolution-controversy.

Chapter 6

Allyship, Advocacy, Access, and Activism

> Sometimes people try to destroy you precisely because they recognize your power-not because they don't see it, but because they see it and they don't want it to exist.
>
> —bell hooks

In chapters 3 and 4, I defined and explained power and privilege and how power imposition and deprivation work to marginalize and deny people opportunities and access to resources, learning, and quality living. But, as bell hooks so eloquently describes in the opening quote, power is intoxicating, and the power of the collective voice for change is powerful.

Power, privilege, and the connective tissues that bind those components to allyships, advocacy, access, and activism will be revisited in chapter 6. Power and privilege, in particular, relate to the development and creation of allyships and how those allyships plan to advocate for change.

Moreover, as the allyship is created, developed, and strengthened through diversity and compassion, the power harnessed by the group demands that each member is a good steward of their power and collectively transforms their respective schools and organizations for equity.

This chapter will:

- provide a discussion about the pathology of power and privilege;
- define more deeply allyships and advocacy, access and activism; and
- outline the first steps of strategic equity planning for change.

First, let us revisit the equitable social change process (ESCP) model. The second and third phases of the model, outlined below, build upon awareness and diagnosis of the equity issues that need to be addressed. In phase 2, the equity leader is positioned to form an allyship and engage in strategic equity planning. Three primary actions frame this phase:

1. Leveraging power, privilege, and position.
2. Promoting, committing to, defending, and supporting a cause or people.
3. Engaging in strategic equity planning and outcomes, which starts with establishing the equity-minded mission and vision.

An allyship is active and consistent in leveraging its power and privilege to address the needs of marginalized communities to ensure equity is realized. Those who self-identify as an ally should be held to account for how they leverage their power and privilege for other people. Their actions should not be performative or theatrical, nor should the actions serve to promote a person's ally resume. Their actions should be transformational and influential. And since performative responses do not necessarily equal action, being intentional in your approach to the work and specific in the objectives for the work is crucial.

They should consistently engage in cultural humility and advance the narratives and needs of marginalized individuals and groups of people. In this-*ship* personal values and beliefs are acknowledged and shared, and privileges are not benefits and advantages that a person should apologize for because the expectation is that those privileges will be used to advance equity and advocate for social change.

Once a strong allyship is formed, this group of like-minded individuals can begin the strategic equity planning (advocating) and establish the conditions to create access to opportunities and corrective action through their activism. Access and activism are phase 3.

Critical to the productivity and reliability of the allyship is the group's dynamics. As has been discussed in other chapters, honoring the dignity of others and acknowledging the authentic narratives of others is crucial. Without engaging in those practices, group trust will be difficult to achieve and mistrust will undermine the group's equity efforts.

In this case, Patrick Lencioni's (2002) approach to group dynamics will benefit the allyship in meeting the desired results. He identified

Allyship, Advocacy, Access, and Activism 91

five dysfunctions of teams that I adopted to identify the five functions of dynamic teams. The first function—trust—mentioned earlier, is foundational. The group has to form a level of mutual trust—trust that they are all working toward the same goal with an equity-minded mission.

Second is the group's ability to address conflict. Equity work can be emotionally draining. Sometimes individuals will just see things differently or might want to approach the issues differently. It will be important that guidelines be created for how the group will address conflict, tension, and contentious situations.

This also means that the group will need to do more than declare solidarity but will have to commit to doing the work. This level of commitment requires clarity, which is why in the first phase, you want to make sure that you are diagnosing inequities based on data and anecdotal evidence and discussing with the team any threats and also the reward of meeting the desired result.

The next step is the accountability of action. Now accountability is also a part of the ESCP model and will be discussed in more detail in chapter 7. First, however, accountability will ensure that members are contributing in a meaningful way and within their skillset. Accountability also means that the team is measuring its effectiveness and the corrections to avoid replicating inequities or creating new ones.

Lastly, the team is working toward success and thus needs to be laser-focused on the desired result. Group dynamics is essential and is necessary for the allyship to remain valuable and productive. It is also necessary for the group to examine the pathology of power and privilege and how each member is responsible for being good stewards of the three P's: power, privilege, and position.

THE STEWARDSHIP AND PATHOLOGY OF POWER

In early chapters, I established that identity, oppression, and equity turn on an axis of power and privilege. Power is a state or process of either imposition or deprivation. It is how individuals can influence policies, positions, and other factors that will impact others. The pathology of power reflects the process of assimilation or acculturation into a perceived majority culture where the members enjoy the benefits of being a member of that culture and where power intersects with position and privilege. The pathology of assimilation and the acculturation—consolidation of cultures into the majority culture is often perceived as superior by those who are members of the majority culture and those seeking membership into the dominant culture by proxy.

This pathology can affect how individuals are promoted into certain sports, guided toward advanced placement and honors classes and programs, admitted into colleges and universities, or welcomed into a community or neighborhood. It might even affect how information about others and stereotypical narratives are perpetuated and grounded into the DNA of the collective human psyche.

Power imposition can also influence an individual's career and job choices, their ability to avoid stereotypes and stigmas based on their appearance, or their lived and loved experiences. It can also reflect the verbal and non-verbal cues a person uses and their cultural agility and code-switching acumen. Power imposition is a commonly accepted but often overlooked category of inequities that can be disrespectful and does not honor dignity.

Power deprivation is the polar opposite. Power deprivation means that a person is using their power to discriminate against marginalized individuals, or deny them access, police their narratives and bodies, or simply view them as unfit for society. It can be characterized by the ways in which some Black, indigenous, people of color (BIPOC), and those who identify and LGBTQIA+ are discounted or their voices denied.

For example, when a transgender individual cannot exert power over their own body because of laws and policies that deny them medical care, or when women of color experience poor quality maternal and pre-natal health care at a dramatic rate opposed to the white counterparts. These can be dangerous, harmful, and potentially deadly consequences of power, privilege, and position.

When those in positions of power also enjoy privileges, especially gender and racial privileges, those individuals are more apt to create policies, practices, and processes that maintain the status quo. Those in marginalized and underrepresented groups are essentially left out of the equation and generally have limited say in what is most appropriate and just for them to progress and achieve success.

And when a person experiences advantages because of their privilege, unconsciously or consciously, they may not readily or willingly critique the system they have benefited from. Ultimately, that can lead to a social and cultural crisis primed to outpace humanity's willingness to engage in humility and equitable action. No one should be denied access to a complete and quality education and should be free to explore and pursue many avenues without fear of deprivation or imposition. Therefore, when equity leaders establish conditions for a productive allyship, they must state that membership includes a willingness to leverage and be good stewards of their privilege, positions, and power.

The other element of phase 2 is the social justice advocacy work. Now that the allyship has some established conditions for how they will work in partnership and engage in ongoing self-reflection, they need to begin formulating a plan of action—a strategic equity plan to outline the outcomes, resources, timeline, and a process to measure progress.

A strategic equity plan should supersede a strategic plan. After all, in education, what are you working on if you are not working toward equitable access to education for all students? This plan is a document that focuses on meaningful strategic actions and outcomes. A determinative mission, vision, results, and an ethos to support the plan are key parts to the strategic equity planning process. Strategic equity planning moves groups from performative efforts to meaningful and accountable actions.

I developed a strategic equity planning template that can be used for schools and other organizations to help guide the team through a process and have tangible evidence of their work. The template and other resources are available at www.parkeredadndevelopment.com. Once the plan is complete, it should become a part of an organization's forward-facing communication, adding a layer of accountability for the team.

The planning document is only one part of the overall process. It also includes the following elements:

- equity-minded mission and vision;
- benchmarks and desired outcomes;
- timeline for progress and achievement;
- evidence of progress and achievement; and
- an ethos reflection tool to determine if the organization is prepared to support the equity shifts and corrective actions.

Phase 3: Access and Activism

Phase 3 of the model focuses on access because of inclusion. It also focused on social justice activism. While social justice advocacy is about declaring a need for change and planning for change, social justice activism is when you are organizing efforts to affect and influence policies, practices, thinking, and laws to remedy inequities and protect the human rights of marginalized and underrepresented groups of people.

In phase 3, the team is in the throes of executing their plan. They might be organizing focus groups to learn more from affected individuals and groups. They might be facilitating professional learning opportunities to increase awareness about the inequity. They could be revising their mission or developing a vision that speaks to the direction of their efforts.

Whatever the team is engaged in should be included in the strategic equity plan and made available and accessible for all stakeholders. This is where the rubber meets the road. Every element that you have put into place from phase 1 to phase 2 will emerge. Therefore, you and your team must take the time necessary to make sure you all have a deep understanding of each other and why equity work is vital to you.

You must intentionally engage in difficult conversations about the inequities that need to be addressed without pointing fingers and laying blame, but accounting for the systematic and structural history that has allowed the disparities and inequalities to persist. Finally, each team member needs to define what their commitment is and what contributions they can make to the efforts. Through activism, access to opportunities and resources is possible, and the work is real and sustainable.

Access and activism involve the following key steps:

- acknowledge the benefit for all and the opportunities for inclusion;
- developing new or different skills, habits, and behaviors results from working in partnership with others; and
- prime others for change and correction, check progress and implicate others in the work.

As the team or group begin to implement the strategic equity plan, they must constantly ask themselves:

1. What are we messaging through this plan and projected outcomes?
2. Have we missed vital information, details, narratives, or data that will be important to the work?
3. Do we have a mission that we can operationalize and is relevant to our present moment and call to action? If yes, then how are we remaining committed to that mission? If no, what needs to change?
4. How are we protecting the work, being good stewards of our power and privileges, continuing to value each other, shifting the culture for transformation, and reinforcing the mindset of those around us for humble and compassionate equity?

In closing, the time, effort, energy, and will to shift policies and practices require people working in partnership in allyship with one another. However, changing policies and practices is the easy part. The challenge is influencing hearts and shifting mindsets to engage in the HDEI framework and activate their compassionate humility for change. Before moving to the next chapter, which will focus on the last phase—accountability and auditing your work and efforts—take some time to review the reflection question and the key considerations (takeaways).

The key considerations and takeaways from this chapter are:

- It is not enough to acknowledge how people have been historically mistreated, devalued, and under-educated. As equity leaders in schools, you must be willing to do something about it—you must be willing to act and implicate others in doing the work with you.
- Forming and maintaining the allyship to advance the work requires strategic equity planning and a team that has developed a healthy sense of trust.
- It is critical to acknowledge and be mindful that each person who is a part of the allyship has to be a good steward of their power, position, and privilege to move the needle toward equity.

Reflection and Key Considerations

1. Sylvia Duckworth created a graphic called the Wheel of Power/Privilege, which can be accessed on Instagram at @sylviaduckworth, is adapted from an image on the Canadian Council for Refugees website. Locate this image to use for an exercise to identify how certain identities and privileges push you into a marginalized category. This is an eye-opening activity that can be used to help individuals on the team share an authentic narrative about who they are and the privileges they carry. It can also help confirm the idea of being a good steward of your power and privilege.
2. What is the equity-minded vision and mission for your team, and how might a strategic equity planning process help support your equity efforts in meeting the vision and mission?

REFERENCES

Lencioni, P. (2002). *The five dysfunctions of a team: A leadership fable.* New York: Jossey-Bass Publishers.

Chapter 7

Accountability and Auditing

> Integrity and accountability are relative terms, and both rely on your ability to self-correct.
>
> —Candice Dowd Maxwell

Part II of this book has focused on the equitable social change process (ESCP) model to guide how teams of equity-focused individuals can make a real and meaningful commitment to address inequities within schools and other organizations.

Each phase provides key action steps, opportunities for planning, and engaging interpersonal understandings that will foster a sense of belonging and inclusion. Chapter 7 will highlight phase 4: accountability and auditing. This phase will measure the effectiveness of the work, examine what additional steps the team might take, and will focus on conducting audits of the organization and the strategic equity plan.

Phase 4 is guided by the following actions:

- data collection for continuous improvement;
- progress monitoring of the strategic outcomes and objectives—this type of monitoring could be monthly or quarterly fidelity checks and is written into the timeline of the strategic equity plan;
- asking the difficult questions to avoid reproducing inequitable policies, practices, and systems; and
- conducting an in-depth audit of your efforts to correct the pervasive inequities.

ACCOUNTABILITY AND AUDITING FOR CONTINUOUS IMPROVEMENT

When you have done the work of shifting mindsets, eliminating inequitable policies and rewriting missions, visions, or procedures to shatter the system, you then need to evaluate if what you have done was effective and how those actions have affected the intended group or individual. A way to hold yourself and your team accountable is by conducting an equity audit.

Equity Auditing Process and Questions

Equity auditing is a process that evaluates the degree to which systemic and structural corrective actions are implemented. The equity audit is a part of the strategic equity planning process and is characterized by five components:

1. Define all equity-related terms for the organization (i.e., diversity, inclusion, equity, belonging, justice, humility, access, etc.).
2. Determine the equity-minded mission and vision for the organization.
3. Apply the definition, mission, and vision to a review of policies, procedures, programming, and professional learning opportunities.
4. Diagnose inequities using existing and available data from staff, stakeholders, and others.
5. Use the equity auditing questions to engage in a more in-depth conversation with stakeholders to address how equity is reflected in the organization.

I developed and curated the following list of questions to assist equity-focused organizations in determining where they need to begin or continue their equity efforts. Anecdotally, most schools and organizations have trouble moving past the first three questions. That inability to move past those questions signals a few concerns.

- Organizations need to address the common language around equity.
- Members have not internalized an equity-minded mission and vision, nor have those elements been operationalized within the system.
- Equity has not been codified in public and forward-facing communication or stakeholders' practices.

After reviewing the questions that follow, engage in the 3–2–1 activity to translate these questions into commitments to practice. I have developed a rubric based on the questions that can be found online at www.parkeredanddevelopment.com. The rubric is not designed to be evaluative, but should be used to assess certain aspects of your work and organization and identify areas of improvement and enhancement that might be used for further diagnoses of equity issues.

EQUITY AUDITING QUESTION PROTOCOL

1. Does the organization have a clearly articulated definition of equity? How are values of equity, fairness, and inclusion modeled by all staff?
2. How is the definition of equity reflected in the organization's mission and vision?
3. Is the mission and statement public and are stakeholders asked to assess the degree to which the organization responds to the mission and vision?
4. How are policies and procedures monitored for consistent and complete implementation as well as any necessary modification?
5. How is the definition of equity reflected throughout the organizational ethos and workplace culture, and how does the culture and the staff respond when the climate changes and shifts?
6. Has the organization developed an equity plan of action based on the policy, mission statement, and analysis of its current equity needs and data?

7. Did all necessary stakeholders—the staff, volunteers, community members—participate in the development of the mission statement and equity plan? How and when?
8. Are there policies and procedures to assure that no individual is denied access, aid, resources, and so on because of race, ethnicity, language, gender or gender identity, socioeconomics, disability status, or transportation limitations, if applicable? What are those policies or statements?
9. Is data regularly collected, disaggregated, and analyzed to determine how staff and other stakeholders experience equity and understand how equity is reflected in the organization? Are multiple measures used for data collection?
10. Regarding the data collection and analysis. How are other language speakers and individuals with disabilities accommodated when necessary? How and what measures are used? What is the data review cycle and plan?
11. How have policies, procedures, or programs been implemented to respond to this data?
12. How have curriculum and/or instructional strategies, programming, marketing plans, strategic plans, recruitment and retention objectives, funding and development directives, talent acquisition, and other professional capital outcomes been modified as a result of data analysis combined with anecdotal and other available information?
13. How are critical equity issues addressed in ways that do not stereotype or stigmatize particular groups? What are the communication strategies, techniques, and processes used?
14. How are relevant equity issues infused throughout all professional learning activities? This would include during staff meetings and other similar type meetings.
15. What opportunities are provided for staff at all levels to obtain learning regarding relevant equity issues and concerns to specific populations, and is equity learning written into the job description?
16. How are staff members trained to identify equity needs and to utilize concepts and methods to meet the needs of diverse groups of people?

17. How are learning opportunities offered to engage in equitable dialogues with policy-makers, staff, leaders, as well as business and community leaders, to develop comprehensive strategies for addressing equity issues? How are these collaborations and partnerships organized and managed?
18. What type of training do staff members receive in culturally responsive communication and group dynamics to increase their effectiveness in working with historically underrepresented and marginalized populations?
19. Are presenters and facilitators of programming diverse in representation and not difference?
20. How is professional learning delivered in ways that model authentic perspectives and narratives and elevate the dignity of diverse groups, especially those individuals and groups within the organization?

In closing, equity and social justice work is ongoing. The objective is not to simply create a new educational system and assume that it will meet the needs of all people. Instead, the aim is to eliminate inequities that block people from accessing and fully benefiting from the educational system because of their born, lived, and loved identities.

Therefore, not only do you need to engage in interpersonal work (awareness), you also should collaborate with others to shift the system (allyship and advocate). You can activate the team to implement the strategic equity plan you and others are advocating, and hold the organization accountable for the changes and corrections necessary to transform the culture to actualize equity in all forms.

3-2-1 ACTIVITY

What 3 questions are most relevant for your school and organization from the list above?

Of those 3 questions, which 2 will create a condition for valued conversation?

Of those 2 questions, which 1 will you make a commitment to ask your team first?

The key takeaways from this chapter are:

- Accounting for change is immeasurable. Once your new plan, new policy, new practice is in place, you must audit and assess its effectiveness.
- The equitable social change process is a highly involved model that requires a team to be fully invested in the process to see the desired changes.

The final chapter, chapter 8, will present a commitment to practice, community agreements for you and your team to set the tone for meetings, and a call to action that I shared with future equity leaders.

Chapter 8

Commitment to Practice and Closing

> We do not acknowledge or critique systems when we enjoy the fruits those systems bear.
>
> —Sara Bishop

The time is ticking on educational equity. The social justice desired is activated by people's humility and honors the dignity of the people we call our friends, family, and neighbors. In this final chapter, I will present several community agreements that equity leaders can use to facilitate professional learning as well as set a tone for team or allyship to engage in operationalizing equity work.

The journey to reach equity is complex and starts once individuals have internalized equity into their daily affirmations, habits of thinking and behavior, and practices. Then those individuals can come into agreement about how best to move forward to engage in correction and redesign, essentially shatter the system for social change.

The community agreements presented below are used in my consultancy work to ground a commitment to the process. These community agreements are:

- Listen and learn with an open mind. Listen to the people affected by inequities. Learn all you can from them and about their challenges and struggles. Most importantly, do the work of interpersonal reflection and unpacking of your beliefs, values, and ideologies that may cast dispersion over your desire and willingness to engage in social justice advocacy and activism.

- Be present and reduce distractions. This work is challenging and complex, but not necessarily complicated. In an earlier chapter, I alluded to the fact that changing policy is easier than shifting mindsets and practices. As an equity leader, you will be faced with many distractions and in order to ensure you can shift mindsets, interrupt systems, and dismantling inequities, you have to be focused and limit the distractions that will negatively affect your progress.
- Embrace the discomfort. The idea of leaning into discomfort has been overplayed. When you embrace the discomfort, you are wrapping your arms around it. It means that you are drawing closer to an equity-minded shift and humbling yourself to engage in compassionate equity work.
- Call each other into conversations. Calling people out will create fear and aversion to change. Implicating yourself and asking others to join you in the clarion call for equity resonates better with most people.
- Challenge protectionism and resistance to change. Change indelibly provokes resistance and in equity work, resistance to change is stagnating. Voice your beliefs, values and ideologies and allow other people to do the same. However, avoid using your beliefs and values as a battering ram against someone else's. Simply respect the narrative they present.
- Avoid sharing your ally resume. Share how you will contribute to equitable outcomes and allow changes in your thinking and behavior speak for you. It is not necessary to offer a running laundry list of all the initiatives you are involved in or the missions you have participated in or the ways in which you have helped those in the margins.
- Share the airspace with others and allow their voices to be heard. Remember that belonging and inclusion are necessary values and attributes to the process. Decentering yourself as the most important voice and person in the conversation goes a long way to making others feel welcome and included in the change process.
- Expect non-closure and disagreement. This is a given. You are not going to be on one accord at all times with your team. A part of learning the authentic narratives of those with whom you are working is to acknowledge their perspectives and beliefs even if those

beliefs do not align with yours. Everyone is in a different place in the journey and as an equity leader you have to respect where each person is on your team.
- Respect the story—the narrative. This has been a running theme in this book. Each person you meet has a story, a background, and a history that is theirs to tell you and not yours to assume or code based on your experiences and narrowed perspectives.
- Influence your inner circle. The best part of equity work is influencing your family, friends, and neighbors. Broach difficult conversations with them. While not all of those in your circle will be in agreement with you, they still may be positioned to provide insight and context to help you move along your equity journey.

Throughout the book, you have been provided many reflection questions. These next blocks of questions are relative to three specific areas:

1. Unpacking and examining personal narratives and sourcing values and beliefs about diversity.
2. Diagnosing equity issues in phase 1 and thinking about the conditions for change that need to be cultivated.
3. Critiquing the current ethos and how to leverage for change.

In closing, *Shatter the System* examines and explores how the educational system is a system that benefits some individuals while also disenfranchising others and what every stakeholder can do to invest in changing the system. Embedded throughout this book were activities, exercises, and reflection questions to help you determine how best to engage others and implicate yourself in social justice advocacy, activism, and ultimately, leading equity efforts.

Finally, in 2020 I was asked to speak to a group of future equity leaders—young people who were involved in peer mentoring and social justice work. Here is an excerpt from my remarks that sums up the passion and purpose for this book, and serves as a clarion call for systemic changes in education (C. Maxwell, personal communication, August 22, 2020):

I have wonderfully honest conversations with people all the time—people who trust that I will not judge them. People who believe that I will give them my most authentic response to very difficult questions.

UNPACKING BELIEFS, VALUES, AND NARRATIVES

How have your experiences shaped your thinking, behavior, and actions toward others?

How do you hold someone's background, history, and narrative as an authentic representation of who they are?

How are you challenging yourself to deepen your understanding of self and others?

How are your views about others developed, and how will you challenge the source and sources that helped shape your perspectives and views?

AWARENESS AND AFFIRMATION

How is this issue or problem affecting my organization/community, or a group of people?

How will I declare, cultivate, and nurture a valued conversational space where authentic narratives are honored and issues can be discussed? How will I bring information to this space for discussion and consideration?

What behaviors will honor this space, and what will I do to protect the space from being dishonored?

How will I engage in sourcing my thoughts, behaviors, and beliefs that create the condition for biases to affect me and others?

What are some of the hidden barriers to engaging in conversation about the issues, and how can I overcome those barriers?

ALLYSHIP AND ADVOCACY

What cause, group, or individual will I commit to support, defend, or promote?

Who do I need to work with to develop a plan of action to increase the awareness of the issue, or to engage in correction or change? How will I seek diversity? Are there existing groups working on this issue in my community that I can partner with?

How will I leverage my position, privilege, and power for the group, individual, or cause?

How will I conquer harmful social norms and replace those with new pathways of thinking and practicing?

What am I doing now to advance equity with my community?

What is preventing me from taking action in my community or organization, and why?

How can I move the conversation from awareness to action? What are my desired outcomes?

One such conversation ended in this response: I do not hold any person currently living in this country responsible for a history they did not personally create.

A part of the issue is we do not illuminate the racialized history of this country and the reasons why we need to create a future that does not continue to oppress others, but fosters a sense of hope and purpose.

We are responsible for a future that acknowledges the history of racism but we also need to tussle and rustle with, and come to a reckoning about, the twenty-first-century definition of racism. Otherwise, the protests, the taking down of monuments, and the historical nomination of Senator Kamala Harris to serve as vice president, the two-term presidency of Barack Obama, your graduating from college—all of the firsts and onlys will continue to trend as symbolic.

We need to take hold of historical threats to our humanity and our desire to create a different and more equitable future. We need to use the strength of our diversity to disrupt, dismantle and to get into what the late John Lewis called "Good Trouble."

This is especially true for those who live with the scars and the legacies of slavery, stolen land, and the trauma of seeing our family members locked in cages. And make no mistake, we all carry these scars no matter our skin color, because we are all human beings.

There are some people you will encounter who would never consider themselves racist and those folks are slowly coming to realize that they have enjoyed the spoils of racist rhetoric and racialized policies in this country. On the other side, there are people who have internalized messages of oppression as being their destiny. Still others sit in silence and complacency. They sit in their arrogance and ignorance, and in their comfortable positions maintaining the status quo.

My point is, each and every person has a narrative, a history, a way of thinking and behaving that has contributed negatively and positively to the conditions and issues of inequity. We are facing a present moment of social justice and social change. That means we all have an incredible amount of work to do, as we are all implicated in doing the work, and we really need to rely on the good graces, best practices, and intentionality of each and every person to do their part.

So, as an elder in the village, I am going to ask you a question in the vernacular of my ancestors: "What you gon' do?"

How are you going to show up? How will you move from tweets to tangibles? How will you stay focused and not fragmented? How will you move from a social media post to a protest, to progress? How will you create allies, allyships, and cross-cultural alliances?

You will need to create these coalitions and you will need these good intentioned people to join you in downloading compassion, courage, and character into the consciousness of the work and the conversations about inequities. So, here is a formula I want you to consider.

Purpose—What are we trying to change? What is your issue of equity?

People—Who needs to be at the table? Who needs to be involved? Who do you need to address your concerns and demands to?

Plan—What is your plan? Who will be the messengers not just a messenger? How will you operationalize your purpose? What evidence/artifacts can be used to support this plan? What solutions are we bringing into the discussion for consideration, if any?

Protest—How do we bring attention to the issue? How are we going to influence others' thinking? Realize that a protest can come in many creative forms.

Progress—How are you going to follow up on your plan, your demands? How will you remain focused on the issue until the issue is resolved? How are you measuring movement on the issue? How will you be accountable to your plan and hold others accountable?

Patience—How will you help each other exercise patience, compassion, and understanding? How will you do that yourself?

Policies—How will you celebrate the systemic and structural changes? How will we use one change as the platform for the next?

Until all of our human differences cease to marginalize, tokenize, and otherize, the work continues. So, I ask you again, "What are you going to do?"

The American educational system is in need of an overhaul. This is without question. For too many decades, equality has been the goal and desired outcome of educational reform. While equality is important, without actually doing enough to eliminate the barriers and discriminatory policies and practices, and correcting the effects of past discrimination, the inequities will persist to disadvantage some and advantage others.

Denying students access to a fair and equitable education in their respective local community and neighborhood schools is criminal and amoral. While there are a myriad of reasons why the system is failing so many students, this same system promotes and advances other students and pushes them toward successful outcomes. Creating the conditions for success, providing students with the most accurate and quality curriculum, cultivating students' promise, and developing productive learning environments where students are motivated and pushed to find their measure of success should be the optimal and common goal. Full stop.

However, stating the obvious is not change. Too often advocating comes in the form of a tweet, a post, or a talking head on a cable news network. While this can bring awareness to an issue, the social and equitable changes needed will happen when those within the system rebel against the status quo and engage in actionable outcomes that affect marginalized individuals and underrepresented groups of students.

These actionable outcomes led and designed by equity leaders and social justice advocates who are willing to download trust, humility, compassion, and responsible decision-making into the consciousness of a conversation and the equity efforts is achievable. It will require those individuals to engage in interpersonal development to unpack their narratives and internalize equity in their lives, understand and respect the narratives of others, diagnose their school's inequities, engage in strategic equity planning and corrective action with other equity-minded individuals, and hold each other accountable for the changes and re-designed system.

Education equity will prevail when the people are persistent and consistent in designing new policies, practices, and procedures to shatter the current system and build a new—a better one that meets the needs of all students. Therefore, the ultimate question again is, "What are you going to do to eliminate discriminatory practices and policies, and how will you leverage your power, position, and privilege to ensure equity flourishes in your school or organization?"

About the Author

Dr. Candice Dowd Maxwell serves as professor and Distinguished Education Equity Fellow at the College of Education at the University of Central Arkansas. She is also an executive coach and co-owner of Parker Education & Development, LLC, and owner of Couture Crafting.

Dr. Maxwell presents nationally and internationally on cultural conflict recovery, the intersection of cultural humility and civility as a de-biasing strategy, examining personality structures for high engagement, and the development of cross-cultural alliances.

She is the coauthor of *Civility, Compassion, and Courage in Schools Today: Strategies for Implementing in K–12 Classrooms*, *Success Favors Well-Prepared Adults: Developing Routines and Relationships to Improve School Culture*, and *Conflict Recovery: Cultural Humility and Civility in Education*. She is also the co-developer of the Culture, Humility, and Civility Training Program, certified by the International Civility Trainers' Consortium.

You can follow Dr. Maxwell on Facebook, Twitter, Instagram, or LinkedIn.

www.ingramcontent.com/pod-product-compliance
Lightning Source LLC
Chambersburg PA
CBHW021800230426
43669CB00006B/145